Tombstones
and
Banana
Trees

A True Story of Revolutionary Forgiveness

Tombstones and Banana Trees

Medad Birungi with Craig Borlase

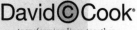

David C Cook®

transforming lives together

TOMBSTONES AND BANANA TREES
Published by David C Cook
4050 Lee Vance View
Colorado Springs, CO 80918 U.S.A.

David C Cook Distribution Canada
55 Woodslee Avenue, Paris, Ontario, Canada N3L 3E5
David C Cook U.K., Kingsway Communications
Eastbourne, East Sussex BN23 6NT, England

David C Cook and the graphic circle C logo
are registered trademarks of Cook Communications Ministries.

The website addresses recommended throughout this book are offered as a
resource to you. These websites are not intended in any way to be or imply an
endorsement on the part of David C Cook, nor do we vouch for their content.

Scripture quotations are taken from the King James
Version of the Bible. (Public Domain.)
The author has added italics to Scripture quotations for emphasis.

LCCN 2011927114
ISBN 978-0-7814-0502-7
eISBN 978-1-4347-0418-4

© 2011 Medad Birungi and Craig Borlase

The Team: Richard Herkes, Amy Kiechlin Konyndyk,
Sarah Schultz, Caitlyn York, Karen Athen
Cover Design: FaceOut Studios, Jeff Miller
Cover Images: Craig Borlase

Printed in the United States of America
First Edition 2011

1 2 3 4 5 6 7 8 9 10

042911

I dedicate this work to my late dear mother, Fridah Boneire Tibamwenda, who loved me and cared for me unconditionally, who prayed for me, and who sacrificed much for making me who I am now. To my late sister, Peninah Rwamwehare, who was murdered because of me. To my sisters Win, Peace, Justine, and Jennifer, who sacrificed a great deal for me. Also to Deborah Karagi, who taught me in Sunday school how to pray the Ten Commandments and who used to hide me from jigger hunters, and to Agnes Nsiganigagwa Bagyema, who nurtured me when I committed my life to Jesus and loved and mentored me till the end of her life. I will forever be grateful to these mighty women of valor who are now in glory in heaven. To my aunt Jane Kasibante for all her love to me. To Margaret Walker, a longtime missionary in Uganda who adopted me and introduced me to the international world. She has been an excellent mother. To Mrs. Carole Nolan, Mrs. Gesine Hoare, and Dr. Eileen Adamson, who mothered me while I was in London Bible College, for all their love, care, and support. And to Lydia Nyinamafa Barole, Feresi Rubuga, Mrs. Tibamuhana, and Mary Taneza Entungwaruhanga, who have loved me since childhood and who took over my life when my mother died and have done all-time parenting and mentored me greatly. To Anne Mikkola and Patti Ricotta, who introduced me to biblical equality that has kept my marriage lovely and exciting. These women have made this story possible.

Acknowledgments

I thank the Lord God, Master Creator, who saved me from sin and destruction and gave me strength, knowledge, and wisdom to accomplish the task of writing this book. Had it not been for Him I would not be alive and well, and I would not have written this amazing story of revolutionary forgiveness.

This has been a wonderful, emotional, challenging, and inspiring journey. It would not have even begun had it not been for Jonathan Brown and Richard Herkes at Kingsway, who saw, believed, and championed this book from the start. John Pac, Mark Bowater, Mark Debnam, Andy Hutch, and Les Moir have all played important parts with dedication and skill.

I thank Mr. Craig Borlase, my coauthor, who always tirelessly worked hard to shape and write this book. May God bless him a thousandfold.

I thank my dear wife, Constance Birungi, and the children, Barnabas, Joel, Festo, Esther, and Omega, for all the love, support, commitment, and prayer.

Ginia, Caitlyn, Amy, and all the team at David C Cook have

been wonderful all along. Frog Orr-Ewing, the New Wine team, World Shine Foundation Team, and J.John: You are great people.

I also thank the Anglican Youth Fellowship Choir, who led me to Christ, and all members of the East African Revival team, clergy and bishops—alive and departed—and missionaries from the United Kingdom who discipled, nurtured, and mentored me when I received Jesus Christ. I thank all my 245 intercessors and prayer partners for their prayers.

To God be the glory.

MB

Medad's right: This has been quite a journey. Yet during the times when it looked as though it would be a short-lived adventure, JB and Richard Herkes had the belief, skill, and tenacity to see it through. Thanks are also due to the rest of the team at Kingsway, including Mark Bowater, Mark Debnam, Andy Hutch, John Pac, and Les Moir. Thank you, Frog, for pulling strings and J.John for gracious and generous support.

Without Cowboy we would never have been able to tour Southwest Uganda in safety and peace, and without Winnie and Eldard the trip would not have had such a lasting impact on me. Thanks too are due to the amazing Connie Birungi for supporting Medad throughout all this, and the Borlase crew for joining in the excitement about all things Ugandan.

This book was written to the sounds of Orchestra Makassy, King of Juju, Taha Rachid, and the people of Pastor Jackson's church up on the hill in Kigazi. Thanks to Jez Startup for opening my ears to African music and to Kay Amon for inspiration.

Last but one: Medad, your honesty, vulnerability, and continued passion for serving others continue to inspire me. May this book help you help others.

Finally, to the Canadian academic atheist I met at the Namirembe Guesthouse … I think you may well have been right: This book really will change my life.

CB

Contents

Chapter One

The Power of the Family

Life is good and I laugh a lot. You need to know that about me before we make a start. You need to know that I think of myself as being blessed with so much of God's grace—far more than I deserve. You need to know that as I look at my life I see there is much that is beautiful and much that is good. You need to know all this because what comes next will probably remove the smile from your eyes.

This is a book about revolutionary forgiveness. And in order to write about forgiveness, you must have something to forgive. For there to be change, you must have something to leave behind. In order to know healing, you must first have received a wound.

I did not think I would ever experience such sorrow or despair as the day my father beat me down from the pickup trucks and abandoned us—my mother, my sisters, my brothers, and me—by the side of the road at Kashumuruzi. We had no food, no possessions, and no hope of a future. All we had was the smell of diesel from the aging pickup trucks loaded with possessions, retreating down the road—possessions that, just minutes previously, had been our own.

All we could hear was the sound of rejoicing that came from the hands and mouths of the rest of my father's wives and their children as they jeered from the trucks. All we could see were the villagers slowly peeling away from the scene and returning to their tasks, now that the drama that had entertained them was over. All I knew was that my mother, my sisters, my brothers, and I were weeping into the dirt, hoping life would end soon.

I did not think life would ever get worse than this. I did not think there was worse to come.

Yet there was. Far worse. But those are other stories for later pages. Right now I need to explain about the road and the pickup trucks, and in order to do that, I must tell you about that day.

It had started the way many mornings did. I woke up to the sound of singing carried in and out of my home on the wind, like sunlight playing in and out of the clouds. The music was coming from the church or the school on the other side of the valley. They always started early. I had never really belonged to either of them.

I was a typical six-year-old boy from a typical village in western Uganda. I had no need for shoes, was naked from the waist down, and was beginning to be aware of making the transition from infant to child. That meant I was becoming more adventurous, starting to move away from the compound where we lived, and finding out what was on offer in the land that surrounded it. Out beyond the pressed, swept earth, I was learning how to use my hands to make things out of the broad leaves of the banana trees that flooded the valley where we lived. I would use the broadest, thickest ones as mats on which I would sledge down the muddied slopes toward the stream. The rocks added the element of danger, and our scarred and bruised buttocks were the scorecards, clearly showing how often our games ended in pain. Thinner leaves I would use to make slippers for my feet. They only ever lasted a day, but I felt like a man when I wore them.

I was getting stronger. That meant I was starting to join in with the older children in the twice-daily trips down to the stream to collect water. My clay pot was small, but even five liters was heavy enough to make the task of carrying it a challenge. Especially when there were consequences to arriving back at home with a less-than-full load.

Our home was halfway up a steep hill at the north end of a wide open valley. Two generations ago there had been nothing in the area but forest; a sprawling forest that, if you saw it from the other side of the valley, looked like an ocean churned up by a storm. Up close you could see that the sides of the steep hills had created land at the bottom that was dark, musty, and alive with insects that fed on the rotting vegetation. That is what our village is called: Rwanjogori. It means *maggots*.

Why would anyone want to live in a place like this? Ask my grandfather—he was the one who first settled here, clearing back the forest and building the first home halfway up the hill away from the maggots that ruled the earth at the bottom. He had discovered it when he was looking for places to hide the cattle he stole from distant farms. He was the son of Bukumuura, son of Karumuna, of Bituura, of Ruhiiga, of Ngirane, of Kasigi, of Muntu. Every one of these men was a renowned polygamist, especially Ruhiiga, who had thirty-six wives. My grandfather's name was Kasabaraara—and it means "one who grinds people who sleep in your house." Yes, my grandfather was given the name of a killer and became a professional thief who colonized a land in which nobody would have dreamed of living. They say it is hard to get a clean bird from a dirty nest, that true change is difficult when you come from a difficult family background. I know there have been times in my life when I have wished the maggots would return and consume me for themselves.

The day my father abandoned us had started typically. The sound of children singing, cups of millet porridge to drink, a quick trip down the hill to collect the water that flowed out of the ground when you poked it with a stick. But after that things changed. It was moving day, and we were leaving Rwanjogori forever.

Or so we thought.

My father had been friendly ever since he had returned home after his year-and-a-half disappearance—which itself is another story that we will get to in good time. Of course, his warm smiles and happy chatter could not fool us, and we remained suspicious—even six-year-old me. But my father was full of talk of great plans and big changes, all told with wide eyes and grand gestures made by hands that commanded the air. It did not take long for him to convince us that our overcrowding was a problem for which he had the perfect solution.

In Uganda, as in much of Africa, a home is made up of three elements: your house, the area immediately around it—often called your compound—and the land that you farm. My father owned a large slice of land that ran down from the top of the hill, flowing through to the valley below as it flattened out. His father had planted hundreds of banana trees, some with black trunks that offered *matoke,* or plantain, as you might call it—a savory type of banana high in carbohydrates, cooked and served with a groundnut sauce or red beans. The green-trunked banana trees grow smaller fruit, but these little bananas are sweet and delicious. You have never tasted a real banana until you have pulled a handful from a tree and allowed their sugary sweetness to delight your taste buds.

Our house was made of mud that had been stuck onto a sturdy wooden frame. The walls were thick and the roof was thatched with dried grass from a nearby marsh. Because my mother was my father's first wife, our house was the biggest, with three rooms: a bedroom for my parents, another for my sisters, and a main living area in which my brothers and I slept and where we all ate when it was too wet or cold outside.

Our compound stretched around our house, and in it could be found our goats, maybe the odd cow, a dog or two, as well as the charcoal fire where my mother would cook. The earth was hard and dark, flattened by the feet of so many people living there. A few meters along from our house was another, slightly smaller. In it were my father's second wife and their children. Farther on still was another house and another wife and more children. And then another.

You could call our overcrowding a form of domestic congestion or an "overextended family," but whichever words you use, the truth was simple: My father had taken too many wives. My mother was his first, but as his anger rose along with his drinking, so too did the number of wives. In one year he married five other women, and by the end of his life he had fathered a total of thirty-two children: twenty-six girls and six boys. So, yes, there were too many of us. Too many wives fighting for his attention, too many children desperate for a father, too many mouths left hungry by too little land.

"I know how our poverty will be wiped clean," said my father one day. On his travels away from us he had found a large piece of land, two hundred miles west, where we could all live in plenty. Each wife would have five acres of land, more than enough to feed us and keep hunger away.

So he had sold our home and the land we had been squeezed into. On the morning of our planned departure, every able body was loaded up with possessions and sent off down the hill, past the spring, through the banana trees, and out onto the valley bottom, passing by the unmarked boundary that signaled the edge of my father's land. Once out on the valley floor we then carried our sleeping mats, cooking pots, animal skins, water jars, and low tables down the track for another mile to the village of Kashumuruzi.

Kashumuruzi was an exciting place. It was the link with the outside world. Where Rwanjogori was home to only a few families and nothing else, Kashumuruzi was different. Not only did it have a trading post—a shop that sold everything from home-brewed beer to pots and cloth—but its houses and compounds were all stuck on one side of a main road that, in one direction, ran to the distant local capital of Kabale, while the other way pointed to the waterfall of Kisiizi and, beyond that, the new land my father was taking us to.

At this time in my life I was not poor. True, all those extra wives and children had put a strain on our resources, so the move was something we all welcomed, even if we did so cautiously. But my father was a dealer in animal skins, and he was good at his job. He was a charismatic, attractive man. People listened when he spoke and readied themselves to follow when he led. We had status.

So there we were, sitting at the side of the road, our possessions piled high beneath the tall tree that gave a little shade in the gathering heat. It was a big day in the life of the local villages, and as the trucks arrived, so too did a small crowd of onlookers. My father spoke to the drivers as soon as they arrived, gave them instructions about where we were going and how to load the possessions. This was a side of him I had not seen much of before: commanding authority from other adults who seemed to lower their eyes and obey him quickly. I was used to seeing my siblings or my mother hurrying to obey his commands, avoiding eye contact and hoping to avoid his rage, but not other men. With the bystanders he was different: He seemed unusually happy, as if he was enjoying being the center of the show, like a magician preparing for a grand finale, smiling to himself at the knowledge that what was coming was sure to leave an impression for years to come on the minds of those watching.

We loaded everything we had onto the pickup trucks and then climbed on. We might not have been poor, but we were certainly not wealthy enough for me to have been in the back of a pickup truck before. We were certainly not *that* wealthy. As we prepared to drive through villages and even towns—yes, there would be towns on the journey!—I was excited beyond words, a six-year-old boy about to experience the most thrilling thing of all, on display for all to see as we made our way to our new life. To my mind this was already a very good day, what with all the excitement of carrying things down from our home and having so many people gathering to watch us. And it was about to get even better.

My mother was a kind woman, and a wise one too. She was also a woman of prayer. She knew how to pick her battles, and she had ushered my sisters and me up into the final pickup truck. Let the other wives fight for the status of riding in the first one with our father in the cab. It was probably best to keep a low profile anyway: My father had been acting strangely around my mother, my siblings, and me for months.

Before the engines started, my father got out and made his way back down the line. He stopped by our truck and looked at each of us in turn; my mother, me, my sisters, and my two brothers. Those wide eyes that had been sparkling and dancing for days were suddenly different. Darker. Narrowed. I did not want to look into them.

"All of you," he said. "Get down."

I could not move. I had received so many beatings and scoldings from my father that panic was never far from my heart whenever he addressed me. Usually I would run or fight, but this time I remained still, frozen.

"You have been a problem to me. You fought against me, and I cannot migrate with problems." He quickly stepped around the back of the vehicle, reached into the brush behind the tall tree, and pulled out a stick. He wielded the six-foot flexible weapon with skill, bringing it stinging through the air, lashing us across our cowed backs. I do not know whether I fell, jumped, or was pushed down from the truck, but it did not take long before we were facing the dirt, surrounding our mother, crying.

The beatings hurt, but they were nothing new. My father knew how to hurt us, and there had been plenty of occasions in the past when he had inflicted pain on us in cruel ways that left scars visible even today. But these beatings at the side of the road were not the main event; they were a warm-up to something big. He was merely tenderizing the meat so that we were truly ready for the fire to follow.

It had been six months since my father had returned from his self-imposed exile, and every day he had been back at home with us he had kept a particular bucket close by. Each morning he had filled it with ash from the fire, and my mother had always asked him, "What do you want this ash for?" He only ever gave the same reply: "One day you will see."

As we crouched there, huddled around our mother, the tree towering above us, the hill stretching back behind, the trucks to our side, the road at our feet, and an increasingly large crowd watching from the other side, my father dropped his stick and reached down for the bucket that he had also hidden in the brush behind the tree. Suddenly he was not a raging father or a stick-wielding disciplinarian. He was an actor, playing to the crowd opposite, his body half turned so they could all see the bucket of ash swinging in his hand, hovering over our heads. His voice, loud and formal, rang across the road as he announced to everyone: "I am leaving my children with their inheritance." With that he tipped the bucket upside down, the great cloud of ash getting caught on the wind before much of it settled on our bodies.

"My children," he said, standing above us with an empty bucket swinging in his hand, "I am not leaving you with cows or property or anything else. This ash is your inheritance. And just as it has been blown away, may you, too, be blown away with your mother!"

I do not know precisely what happened after that. I saw my father's feet carry him away, heard a truck door slam and three engines cough out their lungs like waking monsters that patrol a small boy's nightmares. As the vehicles pulled away, his remaining wives and their children began to sing and drum their songs of celebration. They had our property. They had left us behind. They sounded happy.

We, meanwhile, started to weep. All of us—my mother, my three sisters, my two brothers, James and Robert, and I—wept with the pain of humiliation, of fear, of shock. But as the noise of the trucks and the victorious wives diminished, another noise broke through our sobs. The onlookers were laughing, cheering, and shouting their own abuses at us.

"Be careful, women: She will steal your own husbands! She's a bad woman—she cannot be trusted."

"Their time has come at last! She thought she was so superior all those years."

"Typical Rwandese. Typical Tutsi: always bringing trouble with them."

I was too young to understand all of their words, but I knew we were alone now.

My mother had fled neighboring Rwanda some years earlier, escaping the start of what would be a continuing campaign of genocide against her native Tutsi people at the hands of the Hutu. We had no family left to depend on, nowhere left to go. And now that our father had so publicly rejected us, we were utterly and completely alone. We were like dead dogs at the side of the road, devoid of rights, denied dignity, and completely worthless. The only difference was that we were still breathing. But what good was that doing us? In that moment it would have been better had we died right there and then.

Those trucks were carrying whatever was left of my own happiness. I was six years old—old enough to know that, as the oldest male in that heap of wretched bodies, it was my duty to do something to help us get out of the horror. For my father had taught me one lesson as he had brought his stick down fast upon me: When a man is consumed by anger and hatred, he can change the lives of those around him in an instant. Anger can rage like a volcanic eruption.

As our tears fell to the ground, it was as if they turned to blood. If you have ever been to Africa, you will understand what I mean when I say this. The soil in Africa is rich and red, stained by time and struggles. On this day, it was made darker by the tears of a small boy who wished he had enough anger and hatred within him to change the lives of his mother and siblings in an instant.

I wished things would change at that moment. I wished I did not have to look at the feet of the few villagers who remained nearby to watch us in our shame. Those feet seemed to taunt me, with their cracks and scars deeper and broader than my own. They had carried their owners through many struggles over many years. What hope could I have of surviving? What hope did I have of holding on to life? I could not even stay on a truck.

There is a saying that was written down by an African: "Time and bad conditions do not favor beauty." It is true. For some of us, growing up in Africa has brought suffering and hardship, right up close, time after time. Life has been robbed of its beauty.

Yet is that really so different from the American family that is crippled by debt and held back by too many jobs that pay too little money? Or what about the child from the European inner city who grows up with his nose pressed against the window of privilege and opulence—who sees the cars and the money and the ease of living—and knows he can never achieve such wealth for himself? Africa does not have a monopoly on time and bad conditions, any more than the West has a monopoly on health and happiness. Beauty can be taken from us all.

My father had tried hard to take the beauty out of my life. As we crouched on the roadside, ash in our hair, tears leaving trails though the dust on our faces, we must have looked like the ugliest people on earth. Who would want us? Who would care for us? Who would rescue such miserable people? Surely we had been left to die. We were rejected, abandoned, disowned, and cursed. Our security, our self-worth, and our significance were crushed.

Eventually there were no more tears. We begged the ground to take us right there and then, but it did not. At that moment I wanted to die. I did not want any more of this life where one man could cause so much pain. I wanted the earth to become my tomb.

If our lives are seen as stories, then this was the start of the chapter of bitterness that became my staple diet for twenty years. The poverty got worse, hope evaporated, the future was nothing but decay.

But my story did not stay that way forever. It changed beyond all recognition. Everything that was made ugly by pain and anger was turned to beauty by one incredibly simple yet unbelievably revolutionary thing: forgiveness.

These pages that you hold in your hand will show how a boy who begged to die by the side of the road grew to become a man who was able to forgive. These pages will take you and me back to our tombs and our funerals and ask how God might turn them into maternity wards and celebrations. These pages, I hope, will open your eyes to the change that God Himself has in store for you.

Even today I remember that time at the roadside, beneath the tree, and wonder what God saw. Of course I know He saw our pain and our rejection. He saw the hatred that spilled over from our father and would continue to infect the lives of others in the village. He saw the rapid descent in our fortunes, from a family with a future to a collection of outcasts with no power, no voice, no potential.

But I also think He saw us stay with our mother. He saw us hold on tight to one another, remaining by one another, our tears and cries flowing together. It was a small step, and it did not feel as though there were any other choices on offer, but there is power in unity, power in the family. My father migrated and rejected, abandoned, disowned, and cursed us. But not Jesus. He is a caring God who stays closer than anyone else.

Our time at that tree by the side of the road did not last forever. Soon God brought a kind man to rescue us. Years later He would guide people to bring messages about His steadfast love to us in the midst of other periods of pain. And even after that, as an adult, I would one day descend from a bus at this very spot, my life having changed forever, forgiveness staging its dramatic revolution in every fiber of my body.

In time, everything would be different.

Chapter Two

The One You Love Is Sick

I have many names—six in all. Like most people in my country I have a biblical or Christian name, only instead of Paul, Daniel, or David, my parents chose Medad—a minor character from the book of Numbers who prophesied to his fellow Israelites (Num. 11:26). My mother chose that name. It means "loving and compassionate." Then there is Kanyarutooki, which means "born in a banana plantation." I suppose it was an obvious choice for my mother as she squatted beneath the canopy of the trees, hoping that this next labor would produce the boy my father so desperately wanted. The women who helped her give birth saw I was a healthy boy and said I was Birungi, which means "good things." My mother said, "I got this boy through prayer, and he is from Jesus," so she called me Birungi-bya-Yesu, which means "good things from and for Jesus." When I became a born-again Christian in the 1980s this name gained more meaning, and it was the one people used most when they talked about me. But I shorten it, so I am officially called Birungi. That is my third name. Like many pastors here in Uganda I am also called Jackson.

It is just one of those cultural traditions that has taken root: If you think your son might end up being a priest, call him Jackson and it can only help. My father gave me two names as well—one nice, the other strange. He called me Barisigara, which means "the one who will stay," and Zinomuhangi, which means "they have a creator." This last name always confused me: At times I thought it was a reference to the incredible power of God, but knowing my father I think it far more likely he was trying to antagonize his fellow Christians by hinting that there might be more than one creator. I always preferred it when he called me Barisigara. I liked the notion that he felt he and I had a future together.

In our culture we believe that a name shapes a character. Years ago, before I was born, there was a habit among some people of burdening unwanted children with the most horrible of names: Bitanaki (vomit), Rwamiceeno (be cursed forever), Bafwokworora (let them die), Zinkuratiire (sorrow follows me), Zinkubire (trouble surrounds me).

Thankfully that practice died out with the arrival of the East African Revival in 1935. A lot of things changed at that time, and the ripples of the moving of God's Spirit continued to be visible for many years to come. Years later, in 1982, they would even reach a young man on a bus whose life was in desperate need of change and revolutionary forgiveness. My own children have redemptive names: Barnabas Enoch Kiruhura-Taremwa (Jesus never fails), Joel Elijah Kiruhura-Akanyetaba (Jesus answered me), Festo Kiruhura-Nimurungi (Jesus is good), Esther Margaret Kiruhura-Akatukunda (Jesus loved us), and Omega Jabez Kiruhura-Nomwesigwa (Jesus is faithful).

And so I, Medad Kanyarutooki Birungi Jackson Barisigara Zinomuhangi, popularly known as Birungi-bya-Yesu, or just plain Birungi, would sit with my father at the trading post in the village of Kashumuruzi. My father, Boniface, would be drinking beer brewed from sorghum, while my head would drift down onto his lap, wandering off to sleep as he told me how I was his Barisigara, his one who would survive, his son who would remain and outlast all the others. He would boast about me to the other drinkers, calling me his little man, the one who, though only three years old, had a fine future to look forward to. He would get drunk on the beer, but his words alone were enough to make my head feel like the morning fog that sinks itself into the valley floor when the weather has turned a certain way.

He would carry me home on his shoulders, and I would feel like a king.

I doubt there is any truly royal ancestry within my ancient family history, but my mother, Fridah, was a Tutsi from Rwanda. For centuries the Tutsis and Hutus lived happily alongside each other, intermarrying and barely noticing their different tribal ancestries. But a century ago, when Belgian colonists looked for a way to control the country, they chose to divide and conquer by oppressing the Hutu and elevating the Tutsi to fill all the positions of power. Within fifty years the project was starting to come apart at the seams, and the Hutus were encouraged by the Belgian colonizers to exact revenge on their former Tutsi oppressors.

The genocide that ravaged my mother's country in 1994, leaving over one million dead in just one hundred days, was not the first of its kind. There had been many acts of appalling violence against the

Tutsis in the decades before, and my mother had fled her homeland in 1952, escaping across the mountains, heading sixty miles north on her own to the safety of Uganda. Behind her the machetes had claimed the lives of most of her family. She was sixteen years old.

In recent years, Uganda has been a safe haven for refugees from many countries—not only Rwanda but also the Congo and Sudan. Of course there was a time when people fled our own country as well, desperate to escape the brutality of Idi Amin, the dictator who brutalized my homeland throughout much of the 1970s. I was born in 1962, so I can clearly remember what life was like in those days. I still have the scars.

My mother crossed the border in the lush mountains near Kabale—a region known for its mountain gorillas, beautiful hills, and cool climate. People call it the Switzerland of Africa—because of these last two, not the gorillas. Once in the town of Kabale she became a house girl for the general secretary of the district, the Honorable Ngorogoza, a man who had power and influence. He did not pay her, but by allowing her to work for him and live in his compound he granted her a degree of security that she badly needed. While she was working there she met my father.

There has been a phobia of the Rwandese for many years. There is real hatred for them among us Ugandans, and the common racial stereotype has put them down as travelers: rootless, penniless, jobless, barbaric, backward, primitive. Many Rwandans have been forced to take desperate steps in order to survive, and in those days of exile and genocide there were stories of men handing over their daughters to marry less-than-respectable men just so they could receive a dowry that would allow them to eat.

My father was not an educated man at all, and I have already told you how he was a trader in animal skins. But he was not prejudiced. In my mother he found someone who was truly beautiful, intelligent, and spirited. Being a businessman he knew that at two cows, the bride price for Fridah Mary Tibanwenda made her a bargain.

By the time they married and moved to my father's home in Rwanjogori it was no longer a place crawling with maggots. It is a fertile land, like the rest of western Uganda, and the climate is perfect, offering three harvests a year. The sorghum grows twice as high as a man, its plume like that which crowns the crane that sits in the middle of our national flag. Sorghum is good for making porridge and alcohol as well as for thatching houses. It is not the only crop we have: Pumpkins, red peppers, Irish potatoes, beans, eggplant, matoke, towering avocado trees, chili peppers, berries, bananas, and marijuana are all intercropped, seemingly scattered and sowed at random. In truth each plot of land is well known by each owner, and just as we know what grows where, we also know where the land boundaries are. Graves are often marked by small, low-growing plants that would probably look to you like weeds. But we know how to read the story the land tells.

Looking after all this land is generally considered a woman's job. It is hard work, but my mother had been used to it all her life. Nevertheless I do wonder whether she had hoped for something better from my father. When they were first married, my father would leave home for a month at a time, taking his skins with him on the back of his bicycle. He had different women in the various towns and cities he would stay in, and my mother knew some of what was going on. I do not know whether he tried to keep it a secret from her or whether he saw it as part of his rights as a man. His own great-great-great-grandfather, Ruhiiga, was the one who had taken thirty-six wives before he died and left over one hundred children. Perhaps polygamy was in his genes. Or perhaps that is just an excuse.

Either way, my mother had no right to complain. She was alone in Uganda, with no parents, no brothers, no sisters, and consequently nowhere to run. That meant my father could do what he liked to her and she could never escape. While he was not racist, his family were prejudiced, and my mother was despised by her in-laws, particularly his sisters, for being a Rwandese. Even today many people blame the Rwandese for any problem that surrounds them. Blame it on the Rwandese, they say. Only today it just sounds hollow and foolish on their lips. Rwanda is one of the best-organized countries on the continent, with great leadership that has dealt well with corruption. They are getting their prestige now.

Being my father's first wife, my mother found life good at the start of their marriage—or, at least, it was better than it was to become. They had about ten acres of land to farm, and my father was able to make good money selling his animal skins around the country.

Yet my father was a drunkard, one often with too much money in his pocket, which is always dangerous. He started drinking more and more when he was away on his business trips, and there is truth in the saying that alcoholism and violence sleep in the same bed. In a culture where women have no rights, a man who fathers only daughters sees himself as something of a failure. With three girls before me, my father was full of rage. Part of that was expressed in his drinking, part in his affairs, neither of which pleased my mother. As she heard more of the details about what he was up to on his business trips, she would fight back. She would tell him that it was wrong, that she did not like it. The Tutsis had been the leaders in Rwanda, and their children grew up as independent thinkers, used to speaking their minds. My mother may have been a woman and a refugee, but in her head and heart she was an individual worthy of respect and with something to say. But she had married a man who expected that if he spoke twice, his wife would speak only once. There was great conflict between them. He wanted absolute submission; she wanted respect.

What brought them together initially? My mother wanted to marry a man who was not married to anyone else. She may have left her family's bodies unburied in her homeland, and she may have been utterly alone in a foreign land, but she did have some self-respect. And in my father she found someone who, generally, was a nice man. He was clever, generous, and friendly. He was an extrovert by nature, and short, slender, and handsome in appearance. But he did not want anyone to boss him about. He did not expect that anyone would question his drinking or his spending, his philandering or his violence.

Domestic violence in our culture never goes by that name. We call it "discipline," but whatever you decide to call it, the rift between my parents soon became a chasm, one that was full of darkness. Just as he rejected his wife, so my father rejected the children she bore him. And having rejected his family, he then decided to start again with another wife. Violence became a familiar feature of home life.

Usually when a man takes a new wife, the previous wife gets rejected. And when he takes another, the air turns heavy with gossip, slander, and competition. As each wife tries to shore up her position and gain just the slightest advantage over the others, the atmosphere around the compound becomes toxic. The children are often the victims, with blame being heaped upon them as wives escalate petty disputes in the hope of scoring points over a rival. And because all of the wives and children share a compound and farm land, the potential for conflict is great.

My father ended up marrying five wives and had many children: twenty-six girls and six boys. With each wife we lost him a fraction more—losing what little we had left of his favor, his support, his money. And the more he slipped away from us, the easier it was to write him off. Eventually we stopped trusting him altogether. In time he became a foreigner in our home. And that was when the violence increased.

Our father would beat us as often as he wanted. A week would never go by without violence, and sometimes we would be given extra. The smallest of mistakes was enough to cause his eyes to narrow, his breath to turn shallow, and his hands to reach out for whatever weapon was closest. If a stick was at hand, he would use it, but failing that he might improvise with a stool, an iron bar, or just his hands. Like us, my mother was not allowed to defend herself. She had just two choices: either run away to hide in the thickets of the banana trees (and postpone the beating for another time) or cower in the corner, raise her arms above her head to protect her neck, and hope the blows would soon come to an end. If we crouched quietly and did not attempt to shout or look up at him, he would often be finished within about ten minutes. He would beat our mother until his wrath was satisfied. Sometimes he had a lot of wrath to satisfy.

All of us have scars on our bodies that came from those days, each one the result of our father's anger. If we were late bringing back the water or firewood, we were beaten. If he saw my sisters with a boy, they were beaten. If we dropped something, we were beaten. At times he would tie us up in the granary—a raised wooden structure in the compound that allowed us to keep our provisions off the ground and out of reach of animals. Our father would tie us by our hands, bound at the wrists, hoisting us up so that we were hanging, defenseless. Those beatings were particularly painful, and I remember hearing my father shouting at us as his palms, fists, and the backs of his hands struck pain into us. "Your mother cannot help you!" he would scream as she stood by, watching, helpless.

When my father was beating my mother we would make uproar and call the neighbors to come from across the valley. They were happy to come, thank God. They would talk to my father, and my mother would run and hide among the trees. At times we would know that his violence was about to erupt, particularly when we would hear him coming home after drinking down at the trading post. He would shout and curse, and my mother would tell us to be quiet, strain her ears for the faintest sound, and then send us out to hide. If we were too late and he came back to find us eating—or the meal cooking in the pots—he would kick whatever he could, scattering food across the floor. If he was not too tired, and we had run away soon enough, he might chase us out into the trees. My mother learned how to make a shelter that would help us remain hidden in the darkness as well as protect us from the rain. She would get banana leaves and bend them over to make a small canopy that we would all sleep under. At least we were safe from this predator, even if we were exposed to many others: cobras, hyenas, jackals.

If we were at home and my father came back but did not want to beat us, he might want us to sing for him. He would wake us in the middle of the night and demand that we sing him to sleep. It could take a long time, and even after he did eventually pass out we would sleep around him because if he woke up and noticed that we had stopped we would have to start up again quickly or suffer the consequences.

It must be said that, if a man behaved like this today in Uganda, the police would arrest him. But in those days, there was little that anyone would do. My mother begged the local leaders to intervene, but they never helped. In their eyes this was just a case of a man doing what men did, and of a Rwandese woman having an over-inflated sense of her own self-worth.

She thought about taking us back to Rwanda, but life was getting even harder for Tutsis back there, and no matter how cruel the beatings, they were better than the threat of death by a machete-wielding mob. It was not until 1999 that I first went back to Rwanda, in search of any of my mother's relatives. I could not find a single one.

And so we had no choice but to endure the abuses of my father. I still do not know quite what caused his bile, but his rage was horrific. It was not limited to physical acts either. He also employed verbal violence, using abusive language all the time. Those sorts of words delivered to a child can really affect self-esteem, and for us they added emotional insult to physical injury. I still tell people that in those days it was as if he had a degree in Teargasology: Just as he proved when he staged the dramatic rejection of us by the pickup trucks, he was capable of unleashing verbal bombs that would leave us stunned and in tears, almost completely helpless. It created chronic negativity, and it took me years to begin to recover. Later the physical and emotional abuse were joined by financial abuse. Despite the fact that we were trying to live without salt, sugar, or school fees, our father would be drinking every day.

We prayed in those days. We prayed for him to die. The government cared for widows and orphans, but we did not count. My father was there in body, even though he was financially and emotionally useless. We used to feel jealous when we heard about other children losing their parents, and we dreamed of the day when we could bury him. You must know that he tried to kill me before I was born, aiming drunken kicks at my mother's pregnant belly. Nine times during her pregnancy my mother lost blood. Nine times she thought I was dead. He even refused to give my mother money to travel to the hospital, leaving her no choice but to squat beneath the banana trees and hope that from her bruised belly would come a healthy boy.

There is a proverb from Nigeria: If your face is swollen from the beatings of life, smile and pretend to be a fat man.

Perhaps I might agree with this a little more today, but as my father's rage, drinking, and number of wives increased, smiling was the last thing we were going to do. By the time I was six my sisters and I knew he was getting out of control, and his attacks on our mother were particularly savage. We realized that if they were allowed to continue, then she would surely end up dead. And where would that leave us? We would either be killed too or thrown out of our home and left to take our chances in the wild. Either way, we knew that our mother was the only person on earth who could protect us. We must protect her as well.

We made a pact that if it appeared that her life was in danger, we would do all we could to step in. This might not seem like a controversial plan today, but in our culture, in those times, a child who fought his parent was an abomination of nature. We had endured so many hits and punches and abuses, called for help so many times, and nobody had even once told us to fight back. It was simply an unthinkable option.

We knew that it was a risk, that if we fought our father there would be consequences for us all—severe ones. But doing nothing and allowing the violence to escalate would lead us to death anyway. What choice did we have?

The time to act came one night. We knew he was going to kill her. I do not remember what started it, and it never really mattered anyway. His rage was an inflamed sore that took only the mildest glance to prompt a reaction. What I do remember is seeing my mother—my beautiful mother—lying on the ground inside our house. Her feet were twitching and thrashing like snakes in a sack. My father sat on her chest, his hands around her neck. No sound came from her other than a strange choking noise. She would die if we did not act.

As one, my sisters and I launched our attack. We picked up every weapon we could: a stool, a cup, a plate. My sisters were biting him, forcing him off my mother, who was curled up on one side. They had him on the ground now, and I saw a stick that was halfway into the fire. I pulled it out. I held it with two hands and all my strength as I stuck it into his thigh. I do not know how long it was there—perhaps a few seconds or as long as half a minute—but I do remember the smell of burning flesh.

It was not the alcohol that made him slow to react. I do not believe he was as drunk as he made out. I think it was the shock of his children fighting back that made him pause. Soon he backed off and disappeared for the rest of the night.

We were left with our anger subsiding and our doubt beginning to rise. Yes, we had defended our mother, our only hope, our only eyes, our only encouragement, but at what cost?

Our father went to his sisters and told them what had happened. They nursed him and listened to his account of the story about his terrible children and his abominable first wife. He went from house to house, showing his wounds and telling his story. With every visit, our status in the village slipped a little lower. To the outside world Boniface was a good man—only our neighbors knew the truth about the violence. What kind of curse were we to treat him this way?

Soon he left our mother's house and never came back again … but not before he told us that he had made a vow: One day he would teach us a lesson. It was a threat we did not take very seriously at the time. We were just relieved his exit meant that, at last, we might be about to enter a period of peace. During this period when he was in self-imposed exile we were happy because at last we got to sleep in the house and to eat food without being bitten, and we lived a life without intimidation or violence.

It was a year and a half before he came back to our house and stayed with us. During that time he appeared in our village only twice. He had traveled a long way west and found land in what is now Queen Elizabeth National Park, in a place that today is called Bunyaruguru. It is a good place to go on safari today, but thirty-five years ago it was an untamed wilderness. The animals were savage, and nobody lived there. The land was cheap, but it was incredibly fertile, even by western Ugandan standards. If our father was going to settle there, then he could not do it alone, even though his own family was so large; he would need others to join him, and his trips back to Rwanjogori were his attempts to recruit settlers. I remember him holding sweet potatoes that were twice as big as normal, holding them up and amazing the crowds with tales of even greater riches on offer.

Eventually he came back and settled once more in our compound, though not in our house. He brought another wife with him, but at least he did not eat our food. We could eat without fear that he would come into our house, and yet in a strange way his presence comforted us; we had a father figure around. Now we were protected from other people who might have abused us.

He became very friendly. As well as large sweet potatoes he brought cloth and sugar with him. As he told us about his plan for a mass migration of our family to this new land, we all agreed that it was a good solution to our problems. He sold his land and his cows and gathered the village together to come and say farewell.

We packed those pickup trucks with such joy and excitement. We had no idea what his plan was. We had no way of knowing quite how bad life was about to become.

Chapter Three

Jesus Has Left the Village

In my nightmares I can still feel the fear. My heart beats at night just as it did when, as a boy, I would run away from them. They would hunt me like an animal, using their dogs to track and find me. They would be silent as they stalked me, and then they would release their anger and excitement with cries and shouts once I was held at their feet. Whenever they caught me I knew that the physical agony I was about to experience would last for days. The emotional scars from the humiliation would take longer to heal. They were the jigger hunters, and I was one of their favorite prey.

If you are poor, shoes are a luxury. If you are poor, soap is also a luxury. If you are poor and have to collect water by hand each day, the practice of bathing and maintaining good personal hygiene slips further down your list of priorities than is good for you.

We were suddenly poor. My father had left us with nothing. Absolutely nothing. No clothes other than those that were stuck, like flags on a coffin, to our tear- and mud-stained bodies. No mattresses. No pots for cooking or collecting water. No tools for preparing food or harvesting crops. But since we had no land on which to farm and no house in which to live, these missing items were of little consequence. All we had was our breath, and surely that would soon run out?

In one simple yet dramatic act our father had sent our status plummeting. In the morning we had been a family of wealth. We had possessions so numerous they required three pickup trucks to transport. We were part of a family who could look at others and say, "It is good that we are not poor like they are."

All that had not been packed onto the trucks had been sold. Our land, our cows and goats, our homes—all had been sold to others in the neighboring villages. For three hours my mother, my sisters and brothers, and I crouched at the foot of the tree by the roadside, fresh waves of tears coming with each realization of just how bleak and difficult our lives now looked. We had nothing. If only death would settle upon us at that very moment, then our pain might be relieved.

Yet God had other plans. Slowly at first, like the way you take care when first stirring in the millet as you add water for morning porridge, God brought help to us. He did not restore our fortunes overnight, nor did He transform us at the drop of a hat. That is not generally the way God works. Instead, He brought us on a journey. A long journey made up of many steps. Some were painful; many were small. But today I can see that each one has brought me closer to God.

As we lay there, hoping to die, a man came to talk to us. He had been one of the men my father had done business with, and my father had sold him our house.

"I do not need this house today," he told us. "You may return to it and live there for three weeks. But then I will need it."

I do not know whether he intended those three weeks to extend quite as far into the future as they did, but it does not matter that much. What matters is that for five years we lived in our old home. Free of charge.

Even though God had begun His rescue plan, our journey through it was long. We had to endure the suffocating impact of extreme poverty and the consequences that followed. Without soap and shoes and plentiful water we were dirty. And with animal feces all around us, we were easy targets for jiggers, the small fleas that thrive in such conditions. They burrow into the skin of your feet— or your buttocks—and lay their eggs beneath the surface. They are painful and unhygienic, and nobody wants to know you if you have them. And they certainly do not want you to walk anywhere near their compound.

The only way to deal with jiggers is to cut them out. Using a small, sharp knife you must carefully pry them out, making sure you get rid of all the eggs and clean the wound thoroughly afterward. It is a painful process and one that demands attention, a steady hand, and a good dose of skill.

The jigger hunters did not care about the pain they caused. They were not careful, patient, or compassionate. They were drunk, and they were looking for sport. They claimed they were performing an act of service, but their deeds were those of torturers who took pleasure in their work.

I would hear them coming. It would often be a Sunday morning while others were at church. These men would chant their songs as they marched up the path to our home, and if I had got distracted and failed to anticipate their arrival I would have to run out from our compound with all the speed I could summon. They were nearly always drunk, but it did not seem to slow them down very much. I think it only served to make them more determined and less careful when they finally caught me.

I would scurry away if I could. I would head for the thickest parts of the banana plantation, the places where it was hard to see more than ten or twenty meters ahead. Sunlight never made it down this far onto the valley floor, but there were dried leaves everywhere, and it was hard not to make a noise. Sooner or later they would nearly always catch me when I hid here.

What happened next was horrible. Always horrible. They would force me to the ground. Taking my feet in their hands, they would use the tips of their machetes to cut the jiggers out. The smell of alcohol leeched out from their skin, lying heavy on their breath like the early-morning fog that dozes along the floor of the valley. Their eyes were clouded and their hands unsteady; these are the colors of my nightmares.

They used to tell me they were performing this act for my own good. They would say it was for the good of the village. They spoke of themselves as men who were doing a duty. But I knew this was a lie because of what they did next.

They brought with them a paste made from goat and cow feces. Into it they would mix the seeds of the red chilies that grew beneath the banana trees. They would then smear the blistering paste into the bleeding wounds and between my toes. The pain attacked every nerve in my body.

The humiliation was even sharper. To have jiggers was shame enough, but to have them removed in this way was even worse. There would often be a crowd around me, people laughing at the poor animal as he was given his medicine. It was not enough that we were wretched in our poverty; we were now beasts, stripped of our humanity.

Jigger hunters were not our only threat. While the other wives had left with our father, his relatives were still in the village. His sisters and brothers were a constant and growing menace. They saw us as their enemy and believed it was their job to manage our downfall.

We turned to the one power we believed could protect us: witchcraft.

There are two types of witchcraft. The first is an attempt to protect yourself from harm. The second seeks to bring suffering and death down on others. Whatever it is used for, witchcraft connects you with the occult. And it works. From alcoholism to madness, failed marriages to sickness and even death, witchcraft can be the cause of all manner of suffering and pain. I have seen it work many times. Years ago, when I was eight, the whole village was gripped by the news that someone had called up demons from the grave. Out of nowhere stones would be hurled at the victims—a family from the town—by invisible hands. The family was terrified and called in the local church to come and pray, but as they arrived, yet more stones started to rain down upon the clergy. Once they were inside, the stones continued to attack them, this time appearing to come down from the ceiling itself. Out of fear the wife eventually committed suicide, and it emerged that her sister-in-law had put the curse on the family.

People call on all manner of demons to harm others. It might be a demon from the forest (to make someone mad or fearful), or the mountains (to breed arrogance), or the desert (leading to depression, isolation, and rejection). You can imagine what a demon from the grave does.

We were never involved in that sort of witchcraft, even though we had no love left for our father. But my mother, my sisters and brothers, and I spent a lot of time and money with the witch doctors in the hope they would be able to protect us from the danger that seemed to be all around us. We were sold all manner of fetishes to keep us safe. I remember having a piece of lion or leopard skin that I kept in my underwear, as well as a small bag that contained the tooth of a rat or a mole. The fear was so great that I do not think we ever questioned whether these tokens actually worked. All those things around the house, filling it with strange smells and sights, served to make us feel as though we were actively doing something to make our future a little more secure.

It was never just a matter of paying for the items and then going away and carrying on as normal. You were not supposed to get the fetishes wet, but those that had to be worn could not be removed either. That only served to make my hygiene problem even worse. And at times the witch doctors would cut my skin and smear medicine on me. I did not know they were making demonic covenants: I simply thought this was what all people did when life was desperate.

I believe that Christians cannot be bewitched, but that does not mean we are immune to the effects of fear, and fear itself can drive you mad. When people tell me they are committed Christians but are being troubled by demons, I doubt demons are really there—unless in fact the people are not really Christians after all. Christians may suffer from the effects of demonic activity, but they cannot be possessed by demons, as the Holy Spirit lives in them. When committed Christians are being harassed or oppressed in this way, they can stand in the authority of Jesus Christ because they belong to Him. Their hearts are temples of the Holy Spirit, not of demons. It may first be necessary to determine the grounds upon which the Devil is encroaching on the believer, such as unconfessed sin, unforgiveness, or occult involvement (even in the past or by someone else), and this can be confessed or broken and dealt with as needed. Let me tell you, as one who was reared in a nursery of witchcraft, there is a truth bigger than any curse, any token, any spell: Once we are saved, Jesus commands our destiny. Those weapons simply cannot harm us. Demons do not have homes or bodies where they can stay, and they are always looking for a home that is empty. Once your heart is full of the Holy Spirit, there is no room for demons.

I was three when my father married his second wife. Her name was Lodah, and they were married in a traditional ceremony, the sort that was conducted in public. Having paid the dowry of four cows and twelve goats, my father appeared with Lodah in front of everyone and performed the usual rituals—sharing butter, making vows, sharing clippings of their hair, cutting their fingernails, and so on. I do not remember the event, but I have seen many like it.

That is not the only way people in Uganda get married. Some marriages happen at night when the boy and girl disappear and find someone to marry them. They get fined, but as long as the boy pays the proper dowry it is allowed. Once you have paid the bride price it is a legal marriage.

There are also forced marriages (which we call *okujumba)*, the sort that start out with men drinking and quarreling. At some point they will talk about how wealthy they are, and someone will say, "You may be rich, but not rich enough to pay the bride price for my daughter."

"You are wrong. I have ten cows and twenty goats. I could easily afford your daughter."

"Then prove it. Bring me the cows and goats, and you shall have my daughter."

So these two foolish men change the life of a young girl forever simply because their drunken egos are allowed to take charge of their mouths. One goes to fetch his ten cows and twenty goats, while the other fetches his daughter. She might be working in the field or cooking at home, and there is no point in her resisting. She is grabbed and brought to the other man. The livestock changes hands. There is no great public ceremony, no great show of the rituals. Just the easing of the drunken stupor and the beginnings of a life married to a man less than worthy of his bride.

My grandmother was married to Kasabaraara in this way. Her father had made some wild claims, and she was the prize. She had no say in the matter. How else would you get married to a man who stole cattle for a living and who was named after the act of murder?

But this is not the worst way to get married. At least there is a parent involved. At least it happens in daylight. If there is no father around to protect a young girl, then she is vulnerable. She could be walking somewhere remote, perhaps at night, and a gang of young men could set upon her. One might rape her, even though she is only just changing from child to woman.

Her family might hear that their sister has been stolen, and they might go and attempt a rescue. But when they find her they see that her eyes have lost light and life. "I have already been defiled by this man," she tells them. "Who else will have me now?"

I know this story. This is the story of my own sister Peace. Even today she is still married to the man who stole and raped her. He has not become a better man over the years. In fact he has become far worse.

We were vulnerable after my father left. Even though our father beat and abused us, nobody would have stolen and defiled Peace had he not abandoned us. Life, as well as feeling more fragile and uncertain, was also a good deal less fun, and we had less food to eat. My half brothers and half sisters had all lived in our compound, and there had been times when we would all share our food and eat together—on those occasions when all our mothers were not fighting about something.

Sadly, fighting happened a lot, and it was always the children who became the casualties. My mother would tell us that the other wives were going to poison us, that they were using witchcraft, and that we should avoid them and their children at all costs. The other wives might accuse us of stealing their food, destroying their crops, or spreading lies about them. The seeds of bitterness were scattered far and wide, and it was easy to see them taking root in us all. It reminds me of the saying, When elephants fight, it is the grass that suffers.

It was very rare for marriages to end in divorce in those days, and compared to life in the West today, it still is. But back then the solution to a troubled marriage was normally for the man to take another wife. One or two nights a week he would sleep with his previous wife and continue to have children, and this arrangement kept some sort of relationship in place. But polygamy causes far more harm than good.

My father would always make the same complaints about each of his wives. They would end up being called pigheaded Jezebels. I do not know whether he ever really understood that the problem was his own. He would simply go away when things got particularly bad and return with a new wife in tow. He would extend the compound a little at the far end and build her a house, and the meager resources would have to stretch a little further.

≡

Incest, witchcraft, violence, alcohol abuse—these all seem to go hand in hand with polygamy. It is a continental curse, and it has caused more pain, bitterness, and depression than many would like to admit. The statistics, however, reveal that if you are in a polygamous marriage you are more likely to be physically abused.

About 10 percent of marriages are polygamous here. Even some members of the clergy are polygamous, despite their attempts to keep it a secret. Members of our cabinet have many wives, and at the southern tip of the continent, Jacob Zuma, South Africa's president, is husband to (at the time of writing) three wives.

Will polygamy end? HIV has made it less popular, but the increase in urbanization has made it catch on again, as men look to have one wife for the city and one for their rural ancestral home. This is a problem, and the idea of having one wife for the working

week and another for the holidays is odd whichever way you try to
dress it up.

≋

With the compound now empty, except for my sisters, brothers, and
our mother, there was far less noise to distract us from the pain of
hunger. I began to retreat into myself a little. We all did. We were
faced with the very real possibility that life might be cut short at
any time—perhaps through the slow agony of starvation, or in the
sudden torment of an unexpected death, or by the hands of wild
boys who could grab a sister in the night and take her from us. And
so we retreated.

I do not often return to Rwanjogori—the place of maggots.
When I am in the area, I normally stop at the tall tree opposite the
trading post at Kashumuruzi. This was the place where we were
beaten down from the pickup trucks, and even today it marks a
boundary beyond which I do not often pass.

But whether I go beyond the tree or not, I am reminded of what
the people of Israel used to think about Egypt after they had escaped.
I am reminded of the pain I went through, of the rejection I experienced, of the abandonment I fed on for so many of the years that
followed. A spirit of rejection and abandonment can stay with you
for a long time. For so long I felt as though I had become an orphan
on that morning by the tree. Anger, desperation, hopelessness …
they all took up residence within me then, leaving me feeling so
alone. Throughout Africa the orphan spirit has led many young
people into depression, drugs, alcoholism, and violence.

I am reminded of how deceitful people can be, how they can betray you, how you cannot really build your trust on people. We had seen our father as our source of security, but he had failed us. So what was to be my source of self-worth, with poverty biting at my flesh and the effects of polygamy still toxic in my veins? Jealousy, hate, and envy were inevitably going to win the day.

And I am reminded that this was the time when God took care of me and my family despite so much despair. In His mercy He helped us through. His love carried us. His forgiveness took us out of the dirt. I believe that no scheme of man, no power of hell, shall ever pluck me from His hands. Jesus commands my destiny!

As I said already, that journey from despair to hope was measured out in the smallest of steps. Most of the time I had little idea that it was underway, and it is only now that I can look back and see what was happening, only today that I can discern God in action. He used a range of people, even those who had every reason not to like me.

I have told you that my father's family in Rwanjogori were our fiercest opponents. But not all of them hated us. Deborah Karagi, who was one of the wives of my uncle and whose son was my age-mate and a great friend, was a great Christian. When I was young I stayed with her for a month, and every night she would read us Bible stories. We read through the book of John, and I was fascinated by Jesus' miracles. Slowly I grew to like Jesus, to like the things He did and the way He acted.

Deborah also taught me that if you sin against God He will punish you, but if you ask for forgiveness He will forgive. She taught us to repent every day and to pray every day for food. When those prayers were answered she was always quick to remind us to thank

God. I was only little, but those experiences in her home are the roots of my faith. And I am especially grateful for the lesson she taught me about Judas's suicide and how it led him to the ultimate place of no return—hell. Later on that one story would come back to me, with her exact words flooding my mind as I contemplated ending my own life.

I always encourage parents to teach their children the Word of God. You never know what will happen or what will return to their minds in a moment of rebellion later on in life. Thanks to Deborah I began to see the links between the Bible and my own life. I was a shepherd boy looking after goats, so the story of David was a great encouragement. Even though I was not sure whether my Goliath was my father or just poverty in general—and I was powerless against both—I was greatly encouraged by the thought that I might grow to become more than these humble beginnings suggested.

The story of Joseph was another favorite. Tricked, abandoned, separated from his father, and falsely accused, Joseph was nevertheless eventually restored and highly favored. Could it be that there was more to my life than the sorrow and suffering that pinned me to this valley?

It was in these hills that appear to be folded over themselves that I first sensed God was calling me. After too many times of getting caught in the thicket of banana trees by the jigger hunters, I discovered a new hiding place: the church. The far edge of our land stopped at the bottom of another hill, and on top of it sat a church. The jigger hunters used the fact that the good people were all in church on a Sunday morning as cover for their malevolent acts, but I could turn it to my advantage. By heading straight for the church I found safety.

When I stopped trying to hide myself and looked to God's people for support, I found it. The church was my refuge. Literally.

Once in the church, I would attend Sunday school. It did not take me long to tear my eyes away from the door and relax a little. I found the stories that they told fascinating.

Joseph, David; they were my favorites.

And Moses, too. The priest was called Moses Bagyendera, and he was a good man. He led us well, and after the services I used to go to look after his goats. One day when I was ten as I sat beneath the eucalyptus trees at the back of our compound, I had an immediate sense that I wanted to be a priest just like Moses Bagyendera. During those days the church in Uganda refused to baptize the children of women who were not married in church. The children would have to grow and make vows for themselves first before they were baptized. Nevertheless, my prayer was simple, and I meant it wholeheartedly: "Lord, let me be a priest like Moses."

Thirty-two years later that prayer would be answered.

Chapter Four

Sending for Jesus

It is true that grief brings its own unique kind of pain. To the person who mourns, the weight of tears can be overwhelming. But even in the midst of the deepest sorrow there is the potential for a certain distraction that comes with the rising sun. Even in the darkest moments, light can still shine. As life continues to advance, eventually grief begins to thaw, bringing with it the faintest glimmer of hope and rebirth.

Grief is painful. But there is no ache quite like the ache of extreme poverty. To wake up and know that today will hold the same hunger, the same sores, the same humiliations as yesterday is an ache that stands alone in its cruelty. To know that your life is closer to that of your animals, that you share their food in the day and their floor space at night robs you of dignity. You might find yourself hoping tomorrow will be better, but that hope eventually feels more like folly than truth.

For those living in poverty—aching poverty, extreme poverty, absolute poverty—life is flawed. Poverty brings its own darkness, beneath which it seems impossible to move. The lack of resources, whether they be a pot to cook in or a blanket to sleep under or some land to farm or seeds to sow, robs life of the oxygen of hope.

But that is not the whole story. There is always oxygen somewhere. There is always hope. There is always the potential for things to change. And they did, eventually, although not before every cell within my body knew what it was to ache.

In the middle of his depression Job understood that when a tree is cut down it is right to hope that it will sprout again (Job 14:7). Isaiah also said that from the stump of David's family a shoot would come (Isa. 11:1). Winston Churchill defined success as moving from failure to failure without losing your enthusiasm. Some of those who have suffered the most understand that tough times come and go but tough people stay. After storms there are always showers.

I have already told you about Uganda's beauty. The area of the southwest has a character all its own. The land is dramatic, with the horizon defined by volcanoes lurking over the border in the Democratic Republic of Congo and in Rwanda. I grew up in the hills and valleys that surround those jagged peaks, an area abundant in its fertility. Yet even though in many places the soil is red like the last rays of the evening sun, it can still be rocky on those mountain paths. Your feet get stronger, building their own leather that protects them from minor cuts, but they cannot escape the jiggers and they cannot protect you from a machete.

I was so often hungry in the years after my father abandoned us. When the pain got too bad, and I felt brave enough to risk it, I would climb banana trees like a monkey to eat the fruit at the very top that was ripe but eaten only by birds. Once I made the mistake of choosing the fruit at the top of one of my uncle's trees. I must have been very hungry that day, for as I perched among the branches I did not hear him approach. I did not see him attach his machete to the long stick, and I did not see him take aim at my foot. But I felt the pain. The cut was deep, all the way through to the bone, and once I had fallen to the ground, I could see that it was bleeding profusely. He abandoned me on the ground right there, just like his brother, my father.

I am grateful that a woman saw me. She screamed and then bandaged me with cloth from her dress before taking me home. Though the cut was deep, the humiliation inflicted greater pain. It took me many years to forgive my uncle; after all, these bananas were only food for the birds. Why would he not let us eat them? If we had a father around, people would not have treated us like this.

We call the type of home we lived in "self-contained." It sounds nice enough, but it really means that you share your living space with your livestock. Because we did not have a secure area out in our compound where our goats and chickens could be kept safely at night, they slept in with us. It was untidy and dirty, but the animals' fleas were far from poor: Our bodies and blood provided them with an easy-access, open-all-hours banquet.

The danger outside was never far away. Hyenas, wolves, even lions were all known to have attacked at night, especially before the national parks were established throughout the 1970s. If we needed to relieve ourselves in the night we would have to go out to the forest; even though nothing bad ever happened to me, I never liked it. As soon as we had the money to buy a bucket, we used that instead.

After my father left we had nothing to sleep on or under. Gradually we began to acquire a few replacements for the possessions that were now doubtless being used by my father's other wives. The first item of bedding my mother was able to bring home was a sack, the sort used for shipping beans. It was cold up in the hills at night, and so it was a welcome addition to our home. But it was hardly comfortable. For that luxury we had to wait until my mother somehow got hold of some old surplus coats from the German army. These long winter coats lasted for years and years; they could be a bedsheet and blanket at the same time. When your floor is nothing but compressed mud, lying on one of these coats is enough to make you feel like a king.

The goats' urine put an end to those feelings. Somehow, no matter where we placed ourselves in the hut, their urine always trickled over to us while we slept. Eventually our mother made us a bed out of logs that raised us up off the floor, and the urine flowed freely underneath. Surprisingly, I do not remember the smell, so it was probably not too much of a problem.

What clothes we had were basic. I wore a shirt. That was it. No pants, no trousers, no underwear, no shoes. I was eight years old when I got my first underwear and twenty-one when I got my first shoes. Whenever we did get new clothes they were secondhand ones that our mother would buy from the trading post. These days you see poor children all over Africa wearing T-shirts advertising the Western products and sports teams of yesterday, but when we were children we were not like these odd-looking billboards. However, we did have some strange clothes; once one of my uncles gave me an overall, an all-in-one red work suit with a hood attached. I felt like a man and wore it pretty much every day for four years, from the early days as a ten-year-old when it draped over my feet and hands right up to the point when it began to burst across my back and shoulders.

Even though shoes were objects that had an almost mythical status, our feet were not always bare. The banana leaves made good sandals—good enough for a day, at least—and they prepared me for the time when, a few years before I married, I put on my first pair of real shoes that belonged to me. It was an odd moment, and I felt self-conscious as I flapped about. But I cannot deny that it felt good. Later I replaced these with a pair of *rugabire*—sandals made from car tires. They felt even better.

I was thirteen years old when I started to work for money or food. I would carry things for people, help others brew their alcohol, or spend the whole day digging. I was good at trapping moles, using just a bit of rope, a couple of sticks, and a bit of luck. They were good to eat. Very delicious. And they made a change from our usual diet.

My mother and sisters would work as well. They would dig or harvest for others, usually working from six in the morning to the same time at night, at the end of it receiving a bunch of matoke or whatever else they had been collecting during the day. If they worked every day for a month, apart from Sundays, and if we were not extravagant, we might be able to eat every day.

Did we know life was hard? Before my father left, there were other families in the village that were poorer than we were—quite a few of them, in fact. But once he left we were even worse off than they were. Other families ate millet; we had maize. Some had cows; we had goats. Some started their fires with matches; we used sticks and grass. I do remember that there were some people who lived up in the hills, and even though they had animals, they felt that they were poor. If you were measuring poverty on how they looked, then they were poorer than us. But they had cows and we did not, so we were poorer. Yes, we knew life was harder than it might otherwise have been. But there was not the time to spend fretting over it; there was work to be done.

It used to take us an hour to collect water. We would walk down the hill and poke the ground with our sticks until we freed the spring just below the muddy surface. When the water flowed out we would wait the twenty minutes it took to fill up our pot or our plastic jerrican, and then we would carry it back up the hill to home.

We would collect the water four times a day. Mostly it was just the children, but occasionally women would join in. But I never remember seeing any men at the spring. I stopped collecting water when I was twenty-nine and married Connie, for that was the time that I became a man. Even today when many houses have iron roofs and water collection tanks that meet some of their water needs, there are many, many families who have to collect their own water from a tap (a faucet) or from a protected spring away from their home. There are some men who do collect their own water if their wife is pregnant or ill, or if they are building something that needs a lot of water, but then they will do it only at night or early in the morning.

One day a mudslide sliced away the whole layer of soil that led down the hill to the place where the water came to the surface. This transformed our lives. Where there once had been pools of water that only seeped into our cans, now we had a clean, clear, fast-flowing stream that was easy to collect from, as well as bathe in and drink from. That mudslide was a gift to us, although it has to be said that it took away a large area of land from one of our neighbors.

Water was always our greatest problem. Whenever we were building, we did it by mixing mud with water to make a coating to cover the frame we made with sticks. On these construction days each child would have to carry as many as twenty jerricans weighing anything from ten to forty pounds when full. And since it would take as long as a week to build the house, these periods were exhausting. We would not have to do it often, though, as a house that was properly built would last for many years.

When I was a teenager we acquired some land and moved up out of the valley of maggots to the very top of one of the hills. It was steep—almost impossibly so—and that was a contributing factor in the land being cheap enough for us to buy it. It was also the area where cattle used to be quarantined when they were ill, and even though it had not been used for this purpose for many years, nobody else in the area thought it was a fit place to live.

I had chest pains as I carried the water up the hill while my mother mixed the mud together to insulate the walls. Later, as she and I carried up thick, long logs from the valley floor to support the roof, she slipped and dropped one of the logs. It fell on my shoulder and the pain was terrible. But what can you do? What option did I have but to carry on?

Occasionally when I was younger the day might start with a bowl of maize porridge. Others would be able to afford sorghum or millet, but we were stuck with maize, at least when we were doing well. I generally had only one meal a day, and that was more often served in the evening. During the day, while my mother

and older sisters were out working I—together with my younger
siblings—had to look for my own way of survival. For five and a
half years I would spend the days scavenging for food. I learned
to avoid the tops of banana trees and to steer clear of any of the
jigger hunters who might see me and decide to hand out an extra
lesson in the importance of good hygiene. Quickly I learned to
look in dustbins to find food that had been thrown away. If we were
lucky we might find a potato, but more likely the food would have
excrement pasted over it and we would have to wash it clean at the
spring before trying to cook it. My mother always boiled it up in
her pot, unless it was a sweet potato, which we could eat raw. But
if we found that someone had eaten meat or fish it was a different
story altogether. We would take the bones or the fish head back
and add it in. The water would taste delicious, and we would feel as
though we had feasted on pure delicacies.

On the bad days, the ones when the hunger brought its own
unique pain that tortured our insides, we had no choice other than
to bring back whatever we found in the bins at the back of the trading post, no matter how rotten, moldy, or filthy. On good days we
found good food and called it "a big catch."

But it was always embarrassing, and everyone knew we were
doing it. What made it worse was that we were the only ones, and if
they saw us people would shout at us. There we were, sharing with
goats, pigs, and dogs. The only thing that separated us from the animals was the fact that we had names.

Life in rural Uganda is communal. Even though we were the poorest family in the area, and even though we had assaulted our father and been publicly shamed by him, we were still a part of the community. We would try to have as little to do with our father's siblings as we could, but there were others in the village who were not unkind to us. And when the whole village united for communal events, we would join in.

Funerals were the best—at least they were if you were hungry. The food would be free and often available to everyone in the village. People would let us come up and help ourselves to the leftovers. Some adults would take the scraps to the pigs or dogs, but we could often get in first. We would eat all we could, cramming our stomachs, cheeks, and pockets with as much matoke, Irish potatoes, and groundnut sauce as was possible, and make our way, unsteadily, back home to deal with the inevitable stomachache that descended as soon as we lay down. Eventually my mother made each of us a cloth bag into which we could load our spoils at these events, and it went some way to prevent this severe overloading of our stomachs.

Weddings were also good opportunities for a free feast, although the adults were typically more distracted at funerals. I found this out to my cost at one wedding when I was a child. One of my relatives was getting married, and even though we were not invited, I was there as I had not eaten for two days. I was hungry, and there was a lot of food on display.

My godfather was the head cook of the wedding, and he stood near the fire, spooning out the goat stew to the guests as they approached. I had jiggers and head lice at the time and felt as though I had no meaning in life. We would go a week without bathing and we did not need to listen to the taunts and shouts from others to know we were a disgrace. Our humiliation was deep, but our hunger was deeper. I approached my godfather and asked for some food.

I honestly thought he would say yes and reach in and deliver some tasty meat right into my bag. I honestly thought he would take pity on me. Years later, my godfather told me that as I stood in front of him, asking for some meat, he felt ashamed of me.

"Look at your feet," he said, loud enough to catch the attention of those standing around us.

I looked at my feet. They were cracked, but so were everybody else's. But mine were also covered in scabs and cuts. There was excrement on them, and flies were investigating an open sore. I looked back up at my godfather, and he carried on.

"They are as bad as those of a duck."

This brought much laughter from the crowd.

"And your head," he continued, "is like that of a pig. Will you ever be anybody?"

In our culture ducks and pigs are lowly creatures. To be compared to either is a horrendous slander. People laughed louder now and started to cheer as he reached into the pot and pulled out the largest bone he could find within it. I looked up. What was he going to do? Was he about to hand me something to eat? Were those words just a form of teasing before he finally showed me some pity?

He lifted the bone high and brought it down on my neck. I instinctively put my hand out to protect myself, but I was too slow. I fell over, blood leaking from the wound. I did not feel hungry anymore, but the pain was twice as bad as the ache that had been tormenting my stomach.

People were cheering and laughing, and my godfather sneered down at me. A lady called Margaret, one of the teachers at the school, pushed through the crowd, half carried me away, and administered some first aid. She wrapped her scarf around my neck and helped to carry me home. My mother was worried and crying when she saw me, and I was in tears at the sheer embarrassment of the whole thing. But Margaret told me, three times, "Your godfather has called you a duck and a pig, but one day, twenty or thirty years from now, you will surprise the whole world. I may or may not be there, but one day you will surprise the whole world."

Those words have never left me. Whenever I have felt abandoned or rejected, when grief has held me down or sadness made me ache for the relief of death, those words have returned to me.

People may have wondered what I could possibly become, but I told them what Margaret told me: "One day," I would say, "I will surprise you all." I said it so often that Mr. One Day became yet another name people would call me.

Their doubts only served to inspire me more, to give me the zeal that I needed to keep going, to believe that life was not stuck in this state. Perhaps this was where hope began to take root within me. I do not know. But many years later I was delighted to be able to help Margaret a little. I had become the coordinator for education in the diocese of Kigezi, looking after 220 schools. Margaret was still teaching, and I was able to promote her to the role of headmistress. What better role model and teacher could you hope to find?

My uncles' wives, Deborah and Agnes, who were born-again revival Christians, continued to look after us as well. They taught us Bible stories and would feed us when they could. Another aunt,

Jane, gave us clothes and money from time to time. Later, as I pro-
gressed through primary and then high school, I was able to do so
only because of the kindness of many good Samaritans. These people
owed me nothing and they acted out of their compassion and of
their own free will. I am sure God would have found a way to renew
me had they not helped, but it is obvious to me today that their
obedience to God's Spirit was a very, very good thing. I am grateful
to them all.

   Not every Christian was a help to us. Our house was leaking
and we needed grass to thatch the roof. It was only ever temporary,
especially when we used sorghum, which we gathered from the bottom of the valley. One day we gathered up some stalks that had been
chopped down and discarded on the land of one of our uncles. We
placed them on our roof to give us shelter. But my uncle's wife found
out and came and forced us to remove them. This woman, who
claimed to be a born-again Christian, said she wanted them back as
she needed them to mulch her banana trees. We felt angry and bitter.
It made us question Christianity—just like when my father left and
the church did nothing to help us. When the people who claimed
to follow God failed to take care of us, we questioned Christianity.
When they did not help us with the fees needed to attend school, we
questioned the faith of those Christians who ran it. When we were
hungry, we asked questions. When people were throwing food away
and we were naked and were sleeping in sacks and had no soap, we
expected them to care and they did not.

   Later on some of these people changed and started to care, but I
had the feeling it was only because I had started making money and
being somebody. Even today I wonder whether they genuinely love

me or just want my money. But I never question the faith of people like Margaret, Deborah, Agnes, and others who fed, clothed, and nursed us when we were at our lowest points.

My mother suffered from depression, hypertension, ulcers, and all sorts of psychological troubles. She was constantly afraid, a worrier about even the smallest things. She never trusted men at all. I remember feeling the same way. It has taken me a long time to feel secure when I am in the company of men, and these years of hardship made me bend toward women, particularly as my mother became my confidante and my closest friend. It was only when I started out in leadership that I started to build any real trust in men.

There were exceptions along the way, and while it brought pain at times, school introduced me to two men who helped undo some of the damage done by my father, my uncles, and my godfather.

I was ten years old when I started primary school. I was seventeen when I finished. In those days O-level exams were typically taken at the age of sixteen, and A-levels at eighteen. I finished my O-levels when I was twenty-one, and then my A-levels at the age of twenty-four, going on to university at twenty-five. In every year I studied I was always the oldest in the class by far. At first the humiliation was to be found in sitting next to children half my age, repeating their nursery rhymes and spelling out simple sentences about cows and goats and the sun. Later, as I grew, the humiliation became even more obvious, as I would struggle to fit my legs beneath a desk constructed for children far smaller. Ugandan classrooms are overcrowded at the best of times, and the desks are long, built to accommodate four or five children at a time. When one of those pupils is the size of a grown man, and there are five or six other pupils trying to force their way onto the bench, studying becomes even harder.

Pupils picked on me a lot, and the teachers joined in. They all called me *mzee,* which means "old man." It can be a sign of respect when delivered to someone who is advanced in years, but it was handed out to me with a sarcastic sneer.

Even though I was older than them all, I was still punished along with the little ones. The teachers would beat me all the same, using a stick most of the time. Legs, buttocks, hands—we did not get to choose. If we were lucky it was the buttocks, but there was no real way of telling what the teacher would decide. All we ever knew was that if we were late to school, we would be beaten. If we broke a rule, we would be beaten. If we failed to get a pass mark—beaten. One teacher used to cane us for every answer we got wrong. We learned quickly enough, but only through fear. It was not a good way to learn.

I was twenty-one when I last got beaten—because my school shirt was dirty. They often gave us the option: either be suspended or take the beating. I never wanted to let my mother down, so I always took the beating. One primary-school teacher used to beat me almost every week. We had no soap at home, and the white shirt uniform got very dirty very quickly. We used a certain type of fruit to wash our clothes but it never really got the shirt totally clean. And I only had one shirt so I had to wash it most nights, drying it in front of the fire while we were asleep. The smoke just made it dirty all over again, so my beatings would continue.

The teacher got so irate that it attracted the attention of other staff members. Margaret, the kind woman who had rescued me when my godfather had called me a duck and a pig, came to see my mother at home. "What soap do you use?" she asked.

My mother explained that we were too poor to buy soap. She explained that we were too poor to eat more than one meal a day. She explained that we were desperate and that the only way I was able to go to school was because my oldest sister, Peninah, had married a good man who had money. Margaret cried and cried and cried. She offered to do what she could to help and went away to ask another teacher if I could live with him as his houseboy. He agreed, and for two years I lived in his house, cooking and cleaning for him when I was not at school. It was not far from my own family, but it was a giant improvement in living. There was no shortage of soap there, and the food was regular and plentiful. He even had a hurricane lamp by which I would work in the evenings. He encouraged me to learn, and throughout the year that I lived at his house, my abilities as a student increased greatly. I was fourteen years old, and that year changed my life.

By the time I was nearing the end of primary school I realized I was clever. I was not the best in the class, but out of the forty pupils in the room I would always find myself receiving the second, third, or fourth best marks. It increased my self-esteem and brought a little closer the idea that one day I would surprise the world.

In 2000 I set up a primary school in Rwentobo, fifty miles from my village. Today it provides over four hundred children with an education and two meals a day. Many of the children are orphans, and many have experienced the type of poverty that I did. Some have been through worse than I have.

If you come to the school, turn off the busy road that is used by trucks coming up from Rwanda and on to Kampala, pass down through the layers of trading posts and over the potholed track that leads to our low buildings, and you will see many children, like me, finding hope in education.

Chapter Five

Jesus Delays

There had been enough shame placed upon our family, rolled in front of us like a tombstone over the entrance to a burial cave. There was no doubt that our fortunes were low, and even those acts of kindness—acts which appeared truly revolutionary at the time— were dwarfed by the scale of our troubles. Like I say, we had had enough of shame.

As a result my mother was strict with us. She did not want us to do anything that would drag us down still further in the eyes of the village. I do not think she was overly concerned with appearances; after all, we depended on food we found amid the maggots and mold of dustbins. The reason she warned us against bad behavior was not to hide the truth from others; it was to avoid giving them any more reason to hate us.

My mother was always clear that we should treat ourselves with respect, especially when it came to our sexuality. I may not have owned any underwear until I was eight, but I was no animal. I slept apart from my sisters, and we were all encouraged to respect privacy where possible.

Yet when I was six and a half one of my sisters molested me. We were alone at home, and she called me into the room where they all slept. She forced me to have sex with her.

It happened twice, and the first time was very painful. I was very sore, and the shirt I was wearing did not cover me. My sister knew that my mother would find out, and she swore that if I ever told anybody she would kill me. She told me to tell my mother that I had been bitten by red ants. What could I do? I walked out of our home with my legs apart, and when I saw my mother I had to tell her the story about the ants. Mother bathed me with hot water and took care of me. It took me almost a week to recover. A couple of months later my sister did it again.

What I felt—apart from the physical pain—was guilt. So, so guilty. I felt as if I had killed someone. I felt ashamed. I felt useless. I felt cheap, as though I was the sort of material you would use as toilet paper. I hated incest, and I knew it was a cultural crime with terrible and frightening taboos attached to it. I felt like my sister's prisoner.

And I felt as though it was all my fault. Why had I not run away like Joseph? Why did I not scream? Why did I not go straight away and tell my mother or my other sisters? Those questions kept on coming back time and time again. I developed a complete mistrust of all my sisters, and so our family had another deep wound within it. I developed bitterness and hated my sister with a passion. I learned that defilement of a close relative is painful beyond words. It bites deeper than anything.

I did not tell my mother at the time. When I was twenty everything changed in my life, and I wanted no more secrets from her. I cannot imagine how hard it must have been for her to hear me tell the story of what really happened that day when I told her about getting bitten by ants. After I finished speaking she simply said that we wanted peace in this home and that I should never tell anyone else about it. She said, "It will be a huge scandal in this village. You will be ashamed, your sisters will be ashamed, your half brothers and sisters and stepmothers will use it against you."

I have spoken about the abuse a little more of late. I think that it is important to be honest about the pain we experience in life, especially when that pain goes on to affect us in later life. I can draw a line between what happened to me as a child and the way I treated women when I was a teenager, and years later when I was thinking about marriage and realized it was still troubling me. Although I was less uncomfortable with women than with men, I was still mistrustful of them.

I was involved in a number of relationships that I thought might end up in marriage, but four of them failed, the last one ending just before the wedding. Even though we were both born-again Christians, I was still affected by the abuse from the past and the demons of rejection, abandonment, and my father's curse of blowing away everything I touched, like so much ash.

And when I finally did get married—to my beautiful Connie— the abuse came with me into the marriage. It started to affect us both, even from the time we were engaged. I had not talked about it with my sister, and I was starting to think about what happened. I developed this terrible fear about the wedding night, especially since Connie had told me it would be her first time and I knew how painful and dirty it was for me. I was so full of fear that I almost ended the engagement. But an aunt came to my home and called Connie to join us. Together we began to talk about it all and to deal with the issues. So we started our marriage with some confidence, gained largely by the fact that Connie accepted me despite my past. Yet for the first year and a half of our marriage I hated sex. Gradually that changed.

It was not until I was thirty-seven that I confronted my sister about what had happened. She had buried it too and had forgotten about it. At first the conversation was impossible, but eventually we talked. We cried and we prayed and we put things right between us. We told the other sisters as well, and it was a key moment in the healing of our family, bridging the rift that had formed between my sister and me. It had divided the whole family, with everyone taking sides, even though nobody knew the real cause. But once forgiveness flowed, the root of bitterness was torn from the ground; the broken bonds between us were restored.

It makes me wonder what life is like for girls who are raped, as they get older.

I heard a story about a woman who had been raped when she was a child. On her wedding night her husband got out of the bathroom, and something changed for her. Instead of seeing her husband, she saw the rapist. She jumped out of bed, picked up an iron bar, and prepared to defend herself. She hit her husband twice on the head. He fell. Immediately she regained consciousness and picked up the phone to reception but could not talk. Reception came to the door but could not get an answer. The police were called. They arrested the girl and took the man to the hospital. She was silent for a week.

I know this story because the police commander was a born-again Christian, and nobody knew what to do about the woman who would not talk but who had blood on her hands. The police commander called me and asked me to join them at the police station. I started praying and felt that I needed to rebuke whatever power it was that had taken her over. We prayed, and God performed a powerful work of healing within the young woman. She was able to talk and narrated the ordeal in tears. We told her husband in the hospital what happened, and because he understood spiritual warfare, he forgave her, and they are now happily married with a son. His relatives needed more time before they could understand.

≡

There is much pain within my country, bitterness with roots that lie deep in the past. And you cannot talk about the past of Uganda without hearing the name Idi Amin Dada.

Amin was a tyrant. He ruled Uganda as a military dictator from 1971 to 1979, leaving behind anywhere between one hundred thousand and five hundred thousand corpses. Those who disagreed with him, who opposed him, or who were from the wrong ethnic background were all targets, and his cruelty spread throughout the entire country.

Almost every family was affected by his brutality since he militarized villages, and at every level of government there would be one of his men sitting with a gun in his lap. There is a story that one day Amin called all his soldiers together and told them to raise their guns above their heads. "That is your salary," he told them. And so began an age when the whole of our country was controlled by lawless soldiers who rampaged, looted, stole, and hired themselves out as assassins.

There was no justice in Uganda in those days. The police were corrupt, the army were terrorists, and all the lawyers had either been chased away or corrupted themselves and become liars. I remember soldiers coming to our village to arrest people, and the fear was tangible even for a peasant boy like myself. Once the army arrived with empty trucks and told us to get in. They said that President Amin was making his way to the football stadium in Kabale and that we had to go with them to watch. We did as we were told and arrived to join the crowd of five thousand to watch the president.

Standing on the grass in the middle of the stadium were seven people, heads down, hands cuffed, and eyes blindfolded. Soldiers were lined up twenty meters or so opposite them, their guns at their side. Amin took the microphone and raged against the seven who were there to be punished. Amin was angry, and he made it clear that if anyone else even disagreed with him they would share the same fate as the individuals standing in the middle of the pitch. They were Christians, and Amin accused them of being behind a plot to overthrow him. I was told they were villagers from the local area, but I did not know any of them. Eventually they were given the opportunity to say something. Some talked about heaven and forgiveness. Then the local bishop—a man named Festo Kivengere, the bishop of Kigezi—prayed for them. And then they were shot.

We left the stadium in silence. My mind was split. On the one hand I was heartbroken for the ones who had been killed and full of hatred for Amin, but I was also impressed by the dignified way these Christians had met their end. I thought I knew what suffering was, and I raged against it, wept for it, and struggled as best I could. Yet these people—these Christians—were different. They did not resist or hate; they accepted. Their beliefs were real; all of us in the crowd could see that. It painted a strong picture of Christianity.

Earlier I wrote that almost every family was affected by the brutality of Idi Amin's regime, and we were no exception. I also said that my eldest sister, Peninah, who was now married, helped to transform our fortunes. Her husband, Eric, had already taken one wife, but he was a good man and Peninah was happy to be his second wife. She was very beautiful, and her marriage brought new hope into our family. She took all financial responsibility for the family, paying my primary-school fees and buying us the new land at the top of the hill. In a way she adopted me as her first son, but we all benefited from her generosity: We were clothed and finally able to eat two meals a day. She became a Christian and seemed to be more than just an older sister. We felt as if we had a sense of security. She became the source of our self-worth and our significance. She would stand with us if we had a problem and filled the gap that our father's absence had left. We fixed our eyes on her for everything.

People who had made a habit of despising us started to change their views. They started to look at us with something approaching respect instead of disgust. It was a remarkable change, and it made us even more happy.

I had performed well in my final exams at primary school, and because of this I was admitted into a high school, Makobore High School Kinyasano in Rukungiri town. Peninah had agreed to help pay those fees, and I felt as though life was about to make a substantial turn for the better. Was this what Margaret meant when she told me that one day I would surprise the world? Certainly nobody had ever expected me to be able to attend and complete primary school, and I do not think that even I imagined I would be good enough to continue my studies. To have the financial backing to make it possible was so far beyond us that I do not think I ever dreamed of it. I was the first of my siblings to be accepted into high school; surely the whole world was surprised?

Others looked on at our rapidly changing situation, but not everyone was pleased. Some of my relatives and others in the village who hated us were particularly resentful of these changes, and when they spoke with Eric's first wife, they found a mirror of their bitterness. She did not like Peninah, which was not at all an unusual way for a first wife to feel about the second, but somewhere along the way her dislike joined forces with that of our enemies and turned into a murderous hatred.

Our land is beautiful. I am told that there are parts of China where the hills are terraced in similar ways, as if some giant has sculpted the mountains with a knife. Those hills rise like they do in the highlands of Scotland or beside the deep lakes of New Zealand, and it is not hard to stop, lift your eyes from the red soil, and look up to where the sky is held up by these peaks and feel a sense of God's power and a love for creation.

I felt something like this as I left home and headed toward Peninah's house one morning. We had arranged for me to meet her so she could give me the money I needed for my first set of high school fees. I was also going to buy some books with the money and do full shopping in preparation for the start of term. It was not hard to feel a sense of gratitude when so much good was coming my way.

The journey from our house to Peninah's home took two or three hours. I was not in a rush, just happily walking and thinking about

what life would be like in a few weeks' time when I would start high
school.

Halfway along I met my friend Isaiah, who was my sister's
houseboy. He did not look well. He told me my sister was dead.

I did not believe what he said. I *could not* believe it. Why would
she be dead? Isaiah told me she had been shot, but why would anybody shoot Peninah? She was not political in any way. How could
this be true?

Some people gathered round and started screaming and crying.
Isaiah continued on the way I had come to tell my mother and my
sisters, while I walked on toward Peninah's house.

I spoke to no one on the way. My steps were slow, but I do not
remember much more about it than that.

Eric was a businessman, and at the front of their house was a
shop. They lived around the back, and even before I passed along the
side of the house I could tell there were many people in the yard that
separated the rear of their home from the Rushoma River beyond it.
It was down this side path that the soldiers had walked, and it was
across this river that Eric had fled.

Later I discovered what had happened. Eric's first wife had
formed the plan and had gained support from our enemies.
Together they had raised seventy thousand Ugandan shillings,
which would today be in the region of five hundred dollars. It was
a large sum of money to find, but the hatred among them was
intense. The soldiers had been summoned to one lady's family one
night, where she fed them and paid their money. She then showed
them the house where Peninah lived and gave them the final order
to go ahead and kill her. The soldiers could have so easily killed

Eric, but that is not what his first wife wanted: Only her rival was to be killed.

When I arrived I found about one hundred people waiting on the square of land at the back of the house. Some were crying, some shouting, some staring, while others chatted away happily. They were all waiting for something to happen. The police had not yet arrived to take fingerprints and look for bullets, and the crowd had not yet crossed the line between the yard and the inside of the house.

I walked in. It was dark, but it did not take long for my eyes to find my sister. She was lying on her side, eyes open and fixed on an invisible point at the top of the room. She was lying within a pool of blood. Her blouse was soaked. And there, in the middle of all this blood, was her eight-month-old daughter, Katherine. As I stood there, motionless, I watched this infant. When her crying subsided a little she would try to suckle at her dead mother's breast. Finding no comfort there, she would soon become upset again.

What I was seeing was too much for me and I could not absorb it. I felt the pressure of the whole world as it crumbled over my head. Peninah's other children were there as well: her five-year-old daughter, Allen, and her son, Edson, who was just three years old at the time. These children came and gathered around me and cried and cried, but I was helpless. I was like Mary and Martha when their beloved brother, Lazarus, died. I could do nothing.

I remember how precious Peninah was. She was so very good, so caring, so young; only twenty-six years old. She supported the church, and had she survived she would be so strong now. The fact that she did not die a natural death made matters even worse; we felt as though we had not done our part, that we were robbed of the opportunity to stand in front of death and attempt to slow its advance. There was nothing I did to try to save her, no part I played in helping her. I was left with such bitterness and anger.

There is a line in Scripture where God tells Ezekiel that He is about to take away something he is fixing his eyes on: his wife. We did this to Peninah. We worshipped her; we adored her. We felt as though we could not do anything without her. We fixed our eyes on her. And now she was gone. Everything had been taken from us.

Chapter Six

Our Friend Has Fallen Asleep

I have no way of knowing what you understand about the bonds of family that are found throughout much of Africa. Perhaps you might be aware that we all appear to have countless uncles and aunts, and when you press us for clarification of those relationships, the answers are often quite confusing. The truth is that we see family slightly differently from the way many in the West view it.

Let me give you an example. My sister has a son, and we call him Cow Boy. That is because he comes from Rukungiri, and people there look after cows. Cow Boy is my nephew, but I would only ever describe him as such to a *muzungu*—a white person—because that is the language that person would understand. To anyone else I would say, "This is Cow Boy. He is my son."

Your brother's child is your own child. Your brother's daughter is your own daughter. Even if your brother has abandoned that daughter, she remains your daughter.

You have to understand this about the strength and reach of the bonds of family to truly appreciate the horror of what happened to my sister. To betray your own child—whether she was born to you or your brother or sister—and hand her over to killers defeats common sense, defeats compassion, defeats all natural feelings that exist between parents and children. It is incomprehensible how someone would betray their own daughter. It is inconceivable, brutal, and wholly against nature.

You might now be thinking of images of Africans holding machetes. You might be reminded of the reports of genocide that emerged from my mother's homeland, Rwanda, where neighbors who had lived happily side by side for generations became caught up in one hundred days of murderous evil. Among the stories of killings in churches and schools, there were tales of family members killing their own. Do not think that because Africa has bled heavily like this over recent years we are in any way used to it. Do not think that the trauma and the pain are any less intense. Do not think that we are numbed to grief.

The killing of my sister was the culmination of jealousy, envy, and a long-standing conflict that evolved into a violent hatred and ended in murder. It had been eleven years since my father abandoned us, almost thirteen since we attacked him as he choked my mother on the floor of our home. And the appetite for death was not satiated by the murder of Peninah.

When I saw her body stranded in the lake of slowly congealing blood, I did not know who had killed her, but my mind reached for someone to accuse. My father? He was two hundred miles away so it could not have been him. Eric? The fact that he was missing was interesting, but he could have been dead as well. Assassins? It was possible, but I discounted the idea. I thought it might have been robbers who killed her; after all, people knew they were a family who had money.

I could not be sure. All I knew was that I wanted to leave. I picked up Katherine from her mother's side and walked out. Among the crowd I found an aunt of mine and handed the crying baby over. I did not think twice about it. This aunt would look after Katherine and the other children as if they were her own. That is the way things are in Uganda.

When my mother came to the house she could not find me. I had already left and walked away to kill myself.

The road from Rwanjogori to Peninah's house at Kantare follows the Rushoma River as it flows down from Lake Kanyabaha toward the waterfall at Kisiizi. I decided not to turn left out of Peninah's house and head back the way I had come, but instead turned right and continued along the river, crossing over to the other side to avoid being seen.

I tried a lake I knew of. But there were people around—washing clothes, tending cattle—and I discounted the idea of killing myself there. It was too public, and somebody was bound to stop me.

A little farther on, I came to a bend in the river that gave some seclusion. I used my sweater as a noose and tried to hang myself, but it did not work. There was too much give in the fabric, too little resistance to my neck.

I felt crushed, out of my mind. I crossed back over the river and bought a bottle of penicillin from a trading post with a view to swallowing it whole and having it choke me. But I thought better of it as I held the glass container in my hand; it might take a long time and be painful.

The name of the river—Rushoma—means "the one which swallows." What does it swallow? The word can be applied to either people or things. I do not know who first named it this, but the waters are deep and steady. Yet whenever I thought I had found a place where I could drown myself, someone would appear and I would change my mind. At every stage I sat and wept. Some people would say hello because they did not know me or what had happened. It was surprisingly normal to sit there and talk to strangers while within me my head and heart craved death.

I thought about Peninah. I thought about my mother. I thought about my sisters. They had all endured so much, they had all become so well acquainted with pain ... what use was there in my carrying on? Inside I was nothing but anger, bitterness, and shame.

As I have said before, my sister Peace had been forced to marry. She was studying to be a lay reader when, coming home one night, those boys had carried her to their friend. She had been defiled by the time we arrived, and the bride price was the only form of vengeance we could take. We left with all their cows—seven of them—and lots of goats, but it was no victory and no type of justice. The marriage has never been good, and after nine daughters and a second wife, her husband even tried to kill her with a machete.

Another sister—Justine—was raped and became pregnant, but the man who raped her would not marry her. She ran away and married an alcoholic, but he sold his land and drank his money. They eventually had four children, but when he failed to pay his taxes he was sent to prison and died there. The people who bought the land chased her away. We tried to help, and we brought her and the children back to the village. Years later she was ordained as a deacon and life is better now, but in the aftermath of Peninah's murder all I could see was pain. There was so much of it in our family. We had no rights, no privileges, no voice in the village. Anybody could do and say anything to us. What clearer proof did I need than the corpse I had just left behind?

Could I take my vengeance on these people who had hurt us all? Could I fight back and hurt them? I could not. What power I had was limited. And so I tried on suicide plans like a young girl tries on a scarf, but I knew I was only playing. I followed the river all the way to the place where it tears over the rocks. I was tormented, worn out, crying, weeping; I had lost all my senses and felt as though I had no purpose in life. Death was my only option.

Nature is an intimidating force. The waterfall at Kisiizi is just as fierce today as it was then. There is a hospital at the bottom of the two-hundred-foot drop, a very good hospital that has been there for years. But when I was seventeen, as I walked up to the top of the waterfall and perched on the low wall, preparing to throw myself over, I was not thinking about the doctors below. I was thinking about the many, many people whose lives had ended there. I was hoping to join them.

All kinds of desperate people, from victims of robberies gone wrong to unmarried pregnant girls, have been thrown over the Kisiizi waterfall from that low wall. It is a place where death has reigned. Each month throughout my childhood, one or two bodies would wash up in the foam beneath.

I was not alone as I looked down on the rocks at the bottom of the waterfall. A woman I knew had approached me. Aidah Mary Tasiime Entungwaruhanga was an old friend of my mother. She had been there when I was born in the banana plantation. In fact, she was the one who named me Birungi. She used to carry me on her back whenever she visited my mother when I was a small boy. She was an amazing Christian and loved me dearly. She taught me Christian songs for children and many Bible stories.

She had seen me approaching the falls and called out to me above the noise of the water hurling itself down onto the rocks below. She had obviously heard about Peninah.

"Your mother is in grief, your father is gone, your sister is dead. What are you doing?"

I did not answer, but we both knew why I was there. She spoke again:

"Your mother lost every relative in Rwanda. She has the horror of trying to live without family around to support her, and she was with her husband who mistreated her and abandoned her. But she stuck to you children. How will she feel when she finds out what you have done? You are her only hope, her only eyes. What will she feel when she learns of your body on the rocks below?"

I told her about Peninah and about the pain and about how my chance of education was now gone. I told her that my life was already over.

"My son," she replied, "there are so many people who are educated who are useless, but others who have no education but whom God helps. Why throw away your life for education? Peninah is killed but Jesus is not dead. Was it not Jesus who took care of you while your father abandoned you?"

Mary left, and I was faced with a choice: Would I still consider suicide, or was there another path ahead of me? I stayed at the wall, the noise becoming increasingly overwhelming. I cried and cried and remembered the words about me being like a duck and a pig. I remembered the Sunday school verses about what happened to Judas. I searched within but could find no hope, no future, no purpose, no protection, no security. Life was simply over. Enough was enough.

But I also knew that I would not kill myself. I did not want to hurt my mother any more. I did not want to go to hell like Judas. I wanted others to take my place in death. I would return as a murderer, a killer, an angry man, with hatred in my heart. At that point I think I must have become a killer in my heart, like so many men who had stood there and smiled at death.

It was agony to do so, but I abandoned my plan of suicide. In its place I made a vow to live until I took revenge and killed those who plotted Peninah's death.

≋

I see now that I walked away with a civil war going on inside me. I understand today that bitterness is food for demons, and I can see from that point on I felt like a different person, incapable of controlling myself. Bitterness is one of the most crushing mental problems in a person's life. It is a deadly poison that needs to be brought into the light and addressed, but instead too often we feed it, like a crying baby, holding it close and giving it strength.

The way we conduct our funerals in western Uganda changes from region to region, but in general we will have a period of public grieving that lasts about eight days. In the middle there is the funeral, and on either side all members of the community must visit the grieving relatives as they sit in their house. There are many tears and many, many people around. And at the end of the eight days, the public tears are over.

It did not take long for us to understand that Peninah had not been killed by robbers. As we sat in her house—in the same room in which she had been murdered—and received visitors, people began to talk. By the time we buried her, midway through the eight-day mourning period, we knew that she had been killed by hired thugs and that those thugs were paid by people we knew.

Some people, when they know their guilt has been exposed, will beg for forgiveness. Some will try to retreat and hide. Others will hold out their chests and revel in the knowledge that their exploits are now common knowledge. This is what some of my relatives chose to do. As we sat around the fire at the funeral, we heard them talk in the crowd:

"See them come down from their high places. Ha! They thought they were so great, but look at them now!"

My lust for revenge flared as I heard these words. Could I pick up a knife and kill them? Could I get just one of them and make them pay for their hatred? I was too small to fight or kill, and I had no father or older man who would support me if I was fool enough to attempt it. So I chose otherwise. I chose to avoid them at all costs, to never visit them again, and to curse the day I was born. They had murdered my sister, and in my heart I had killed them, too.

But that was not the end of it. Gradually I started to dwell on another thought: What if they wanted to kill me as well? Why stop at Peninah? Why did I think this was the end of the matter?

My past was dark. My future was dark. My present was nothing like it was supposed to be. I had gained a place at high school, but without the funds to cover the fees and other costs, I was left with no option but to stay at home. Eric had no more contact with us. On the instruction of their employers, the soldiers had warned him not to continue supporting my mother, and he stuck to their instructions. I had no status in society; my age-mates had long since started at high school and even completed it. They had moved on, yet I remained. Strangers seemed to despise me. Even the trees laughed at me. I felt abandoned; first my father, and now this. Nobody was there alongside me, and the only voices I could hear were of those who taunted us for our short-lived improvement in fortunes.

My plan was clear. I made a list of the people I would kill in order to avenge the death of my sister and the betrayal by our father. The list had nineteen names on it. All I needed was some time and a gun, and I would wipe them out.

As my younger classmates went off to high school, I stayed at home. For a whole year it was very difficult. I felt unloved, cheap, and small. I was dying every day, thinking about school all the time. It was as if the real me died that year. Slowly, through a thousand cuts, my empty life was locked into a cycle that served only to remind me of my father's brutality.

My self-esteem was completely crushed, the pain even more acute as the sight of schoolboys reminded me that I was not an academic failure but a financial one. I felt hated, rejected, useless, without purpose. I remembered all the things people had said about me and went into a deep depression. It caused me to drink heavily, but whenever I was sober I could see that the problems were just the same.

I developed a volcanic anger, such that anything small made me fly off into a rage. In a way I believe I lost my mind. At times I would become so distracted by my inner civil war that I would miss a particular turn I was meant to take and end up a mile or two away from where I wanted to be. I would talk to myself as I walked, ranting in particular about my father. Even later on in life I would have anniversaries of bitterness, and whenever a significant date came around, like Peninah's death or the time our father left us, I would go back into the depression.

I heard that my father and his wives and children celebrated my sister's funeral. My anger only increased. Two of my brothers, James and Robert, fell into such a depression after my sister's death that they became alcoholics and later died because of it; James died of liver cancer and Robert died of alimentary canal cancer. The story of the impact of my sister's brutal murder on my sisters and brothers would fill another book.

The pain did not stop. Some of my sisters were raped during this time, and it was devastating. I was enraged yet powerless. I knew the people in my village who were attacking them, but I could do nothing to stop it. They used my sisters as toilet paper. The Bakiga (my tribe) was a male-dominated society, fiercely patriarchal. The cultural laws favor and defend men while supporting the oppression of women. Women are treated as second class, and because a dowry is paid before marriage, many are treated like property. They are oppressed, enslaved, segregated, and treated as beasts of burden. They are sex machines without rights, not empowered financially, intellectually, or politically. They are vulnerable and exposed; domestic violence against women is so deep—even in Christian homes—that there is no political will to stop it. We would need another book to talk about that as well.

It was such a hard year in my life, and it set in motion the habits of a destructive lifestyle: drinking, being angry, shouting at people, not greeting them, killing people in my heart, seeing death all around, spending energy I had within me on vowing to kill.

My behavior began to have an impact on the rest of my family, so much so that eventually my mother devised an audacious plan to transform me. She would work even harder than she had been—as if that were possible—and raise the money to send me to school. She worked so hard, as did my sisters and brothers. They dug crops, they brewed alcohol, and they sold whatever they could to raise money. My sisters even prostituted themselves. I will never forget the sacrifice they made for my education.

They had nobody to defend them, and they were fighting to improve life for somebody else. They made so many sacrifices that invited such pain into their lives. I did what I could, raising money by trapping moles or burning charcoal. Within a year we had raised enough money to send me to school.

You cannot fight the sort of shame or humiliation that comes from prostitution. Some of my sisters became pregnant and some had abortions. Their actions showed me that I was not alone, but it also reinforced my understanding of the world as a place where pain, suffering, and abuse were as omnipresent as the hills that hemmed us in.

As for me, I was a powder keg. Later I gained a glimpse of my future. I met some soldiers fighting to support the exiled opponent of Idi Amin, a man called Milton Obote. I joined the youth wing of his party and was told that if I completed my studies, I could join the army, where I would be given my own gun. This was it, the key to my plan. Once I had a gun and a soldier's badge, I could work my way through my list, from one to nineteen. The blood would flow and justice would be done. This was how I would gain revenge.

Chapter Seven

If Only He Had Been Here Sooner

It is a long way from Rwanjogori to Rukungiri—sixty-five miles in all. From the ridge above the spring near our house, you have to scan the horizon and look to the hills in the west. Between two of the smaller peaks is a road that is invisible from home, but it is there. That road was where my walk to high school began.

My fellow travelers along the road were similar to those you might see today: mothers with children strapped to their backs; young men pushing bicycles loaded with impossibly heavy loads—from child-sized bunches of matoke balanced on long poles, to multiple jerricans of water with a weight of up to 220 pounds; old men in secondhand suits that must have lived such very different lives on the backs of their first wearers.

At times when I am with *muzungu* in western Uganda they ask how it is that we seem to know one another. Having lived in the United Kingdom I can give you a clear answer: We *seem* to know one another because we *do* know one another, and we know one another because we spend more time talking to one another than Westerners do.

When I was an adult I would often walk the eighteen miles from Kabale to our home in Rwanjogori. Halfway along is the hill that we call *mutagamba*—meaning "do not talk." The hill is so steep that all your breath must be conserved to power legs and lungs, and the burning in your calves starts long before you can even think about looking for the summit. But once you reach the top the view is spectacular, and I would always stop there to drink some water and eat. There would be others there as well, and even if we did not immediately know one another we would shake hands and share what we had. It is hard to consider someone a stranger when you eat with him.

My journey to school was always on foot. Bare feet. I would carry all I needed for the term ahead: a few books, some clothes, water and food for the journey, and—twice a year—a mattress. It was a heavy load, and the walk would take a little over sixteen hours. It was mildly less exhausting to walk it at night. Less exhausting, perhaps, but not less dangerous. Once when I was walking home in the moonlight along with a group of friends, we came across a hippo. Fifteen of us, all too poor to get the bus, walking with our suitcases, and there was a hippo. If you have ever been on safari you will have heard how in Africa, most years hippos claim more lives than lions. They are mammoth beasts and will charge at anything that gets in between them and the water in which they wallow. We all dropped our bags and ran, only to return once it had gone.

Another time walking home I was foolish and grabbed a stick of sugar cane. I chewed it for miles, enjoying the sweetness that gave me a little extra energy. I forgot that sugar cane was a favorite place for female mosquitoes to lay their eggs. Without knowing it I was eating malarial eggs. Within a few days of arriving back at home I started feeling uneasy, then a little sick. Eventually I lost my senses and was at risk of contracting cerebral malaria, from which there is no full recovery. I came to and found my grandmother crying. She thought I had died.

The first time I walked to Makobore High School in Rukungiri my mother came along too. I had no mattress, no bedsheets, no shoes, no trousers—just a spare set of clothes and provisions for the journey—but I was happy. Most women in Uganda still wear a brightly colored cloth that has many uses—warmth, protection from the elements, carrying loads—and my mother used hers to make me a sort of mattress. It was like a sleeping bag, and when I reached school I could fill it with dry grass. At the end of the term I threw the grass out and took the bag home.

My mother joined me on that first journey so that we could talk. I remember only this of our conversation:

"Do not do anything to bring further shame on our family."

"Yes, mother."

I loved my mother so much. She died a few years ago, and I am glad to say that although I did not honor the promise I made to her that day, she and I were always close. When the time came for me to confess all the ways in which I had brought shame upon her, she was gracious, loving, and forgiving.

Once we arrived at the school on that first journey, she spoke with the head teacher, Mr. Stanley Munabi, who was a good man. She told him about the troubles we had been through as a family: Peninah's murder, my suicide attempts, the abandonment by my father, as well as how he had not even returned home when Peninah was buried.

She had raised enough money for the basic school fees but not enough for my board and lodging. She pleaded with him to take me in.

"Well," said the headmaster, "if he is hardworking I will give him jobs. He can earn his keep that way."

Like I said, the headmaster was a good man.

So I started. I turned my hand to whatever manual jobs needed doing. I would dig pit latrines and make temporary kitchens out of stones and iron grills; I would wash dishes, cut the grass, dig the gardens, wash the school truck. Some of these jobs I carried on throughout my years there. My mother would add in what money she could, and eventually one of my older sisters, Winnie, got married and moved to Rukungiri, just a few miles away from the school, so I would go there to eat and borrow money when I needed it. Winnie's husband and mother- and father-in-law were very helpful, and I count them as good friends today.

But I was not behaving well. At the same time I was making a good impression on the headmaster I also developed a second life that I kept hidden from him, and from my mother and family, too. I was drinking heavily. It would give me temporary happiness, but it soon turned to an addiction. And because addicts need others around them, I found others who also liked to drink. They were a group called the Kibanda Boys, a gang who were pretty rough. Together we were drinkers, but we were also dancers and fighters.

We would go to villages whenever there was a wedding and start a fight. We would take the same type of violent red peppers that the jigger hunters had used on my own agonized wounds and would crush them up to be thrown onto the floor where people danced.

It would not take long before the dancers' feet mixed up the chili with the dust, rising to form a cloud which, when inhaled, was very painful. The dance would be ruined and we would be happy.

The gang had a terrible reputation. Before I joined, there was one fight with a village that had started when a woman was accused of bewitching a member of the school staff, who had died. The gang called up half the school to join in and led the mob to her house, where it was rumored that they beat her to death. There was also a story that they had stoned to death a member of the staff as well as killed a policeman who got caught up in a scuffle. I had not arrived at the school at this time, but I was there when we invaded a nearby girls' school—not just once, but more than three or four times. The girls were beaten and raped. Peer pressure is a big thing—you want to please people—so I would get a stick and join in the beating, though nothing more. At those times I may not have known why I was fighting, but I knew I needed to do it to keep my place.

All the boys in the gang shared the same background and the same passion for alcohol. They protected me from being bullied and helped me out when I did not have enough money to buy drink. And we would walk to our homes together—most of the nineteen of us. They were not as poor as I was, but they would far rather spend their money on alcohol than on a bus fare.

I had such anger and bitterness in my heart that it did not take much for me to start to become violent. Without even asking questions I would go and do what I was told. I was a drunken mess: wetting my bed, vomiting in my half sleep, and running up drinking debts that I had no means of ever paying. To get out of the worst of them I would steal books, plates, and spoons to go and sell.

We often raged against the school, but one time we fought with greater force than usual. We were angry because the bursar had been stealing from the pupils. He would deny having any knowledge of receiving payment for fees, and if you had lost your receipt you had little choice but to pay again. The food was also not good, and because it was nearing the end of term we had examinations fever. This was cause enough for us to unleash the full chaos of our violence. We smashed windows, set fire to the bursar's house, trashed other staff houses, and destroyed school property. It was a moment of pure violence, and we loved it.

And yet I was like an orphan there, being favored by the school, working hard for the headmaster, behaving in such an exemplary way while working for him that he never believed anyone who accused me of being involved. He stood by me. And yet, in secret, I was a thug.

I felt guilty, but it was not until I became a Christian that I knew quite how wrong my actions had been. The thing I most regret about the time in the gang was that riot. As well as the buildings we also attacked many people. We beat many younger students and stole their money; we also attacked nearby shops and looted money and property. Dozens of policemen came and we threw stones at them and they beat us and shot in the air and many students were arrested. We ran through nearby villages, vandalizing property, beating the residents, and looting shops and bars. We took all the beer we could find.

The headmaster feared the gang. He never brought it up with me, although after the riot he called me in.

"People are saying you were involved," he asked. "Were you?"

My denial was dramatic; I lay on the ground, wept, and swore I had no involvement in any of it at all.

He defended me in front of the staff and board of governors, but it was not enough to get me off the charges completely. We were all sent home and forced to pay for the damages—three thousand Ugandan shillings, which was a lot of money in those days, more like two hundred dollars today. It will not surprise you to learn that I did not tell my mother about this.

In 1982, three years after Peninah's murder and two years after I started at Makobore High School, a Christian choir from Makerere University, Kampala, came to sing. They were called the Anglican Youth Fellowship choir, and they were more of a band than a simple choir. They had guitars and drums and keyboards and all the rest. Because we were a boys' school we were happy about any girls coming over to see us, and as a gang we agreed to go along to hear them perform and join in the dancing. But we also agreed that, if they preached, we would shout at the tops of our voices and unleash our chaos on them.

Our school was a notorious school with a culture of violence, and the staff told the choir our intentions. Understandably the choir decided that they would not preach but that they would simply introduce the songs. One of them, a young woman called Christine, started up:

"We are going to sing a song about love. But before we start we want to tell you that God loves you unconditionally. His love for you does not depend on who you are, where you come from, your background, what you have done. He just loves you the way you are, because He made you in His own image. He can be your security.

Do you know that your source of true security is from God? Your father, your mother, your sisters, your brothers are not your security. Your education is not your source of security. Even politics is not your security. Idi Amin said he was president for life, but where is he now?"

Christine was a very beautiful girl, very confident as well. We used to think that only ugly, poor, frustrated, and troubled people became born-again Christians. I thought Christianity was dull, but these young people were excited and confident. We were listening.

"Some of you have been abandoned by your fathers, some of you are victims of domestic violence, but God's love for you is unconditional and it can be your source of security and self-worth. God can be the source of a sense of your own value; while you are students today, you may well be cabinet ministers, presidents, or major-generals tomorrow. God values you and you are precious to Him, and you have a purpose. You were born a boy not by accident. You have a purpose. God is the true source of your security, your self-worth, and your significance. Receive Him now. Believe in Him now. Trust your lives and destiny to Him now, and your lives will never be the same. Jesus saves, He keeps, and He satisfies. He is a good guy. God is a dependable, caring, close, and loving Father. Boys, I am telling you this: He will never let you down!"

It was as if she was speaking directly to me. Even down to that part about not being a boy by accident. I had never told anyone this, but at times in my life I had even wished I had been born a girl. At least then I could have taken a job as a maid and then married, so that someone would look after me.

I stood in the crowd in the yard in front of the school gates and wanted to disappear. I could have evaporated; I would have let my life be carried away on the breeze right then, in order to avoid the challenge inhabiting that moment.

But Christine had stopped talking, and in the silence that filled me I sensed a drop of love enter my heart. It was like that small sip of perfectly cold water on a hot day; not enough to quench, but enough to arrest discomfort, if only for a moment.

Soon there came a question within me: If she really was speaking the truth, and God really did love me as she said, why did God allow all this suffering to happen to me? Why?

But my heart felt another touch of warmth. The question faded in its importance. What mattered was another question that rose up as I looked in: Where was my security? My father? He had let me down. My sisters? One had been murdered and another had molested me. My uncles, aunts, and cousins? Most of them were not helpful at all, and I still feared that some of them wanted me dead. I felt that so many people had used and exploited me in different ways. I realized that, apart from my mother, I had no one around who loved me unconditionally. For the first time I doubted whether her love was enough. Look how I had treated her: After all she had done for me, after all the promises I had made to her, my life had become a rage and an embarrassment to her. I had let her down. What self-respect could I have if I treated the only one who truly cared for me like this?

My self-esteem had been crushed when my father left, and I wept. I looked at these boys and girls as they sang, and they were happy, joyful, united. They were my age-mates, and yet they were all at university while I was struggling to learn how to read. I admired them. In my heart I whispered the simplest of words: "I wish I was like them."

The words may have been simple, but they were significant. As the choir kept on singing I was now open to all they said. I was thirsty, and they were a fountain at which I could finally satisfy my thirst.

A boy called Abraham stepped up at the end of the song to introduce another song:

"Christine told you that God loves you unconditionally, but He also forgives you unconditionally and can wipe clean every sin you have ever committed. No matter how bad you have been, He can forgive. That is why He died on the cross. He can forgive you—just like He forgave Saul and all those other murderers and fornicators. He can forgive every sin if you are willing to confess to Him today. Some of you are thieves who have been stealing books; others are drinking heavily, involved in witchcraft, the occult, violence, sexual immorality. Some of you are contemplating suicide or planning to kill someone. But Jesus is here today to forgive."

With that, Abraham introduced a song about forgiveness, singing, "What can take away my sin? Nothing but the blood of Jesus." While they sang I asked myself, "Can God really forgive me?" I had a small notebook with a list of nineteen people in it, their crimes against me listed alongside their names. Every year I would celebrate anniversaries of evil—the horrors done to me. I was in a notorious gang, and most people knew it. My mother had been called in to see the headmaster because he wanted to suspend me after all the drinking, which was against the school rules. He had caught and warned me many times but had never believed people who had accused me of greater crimes. Yet students were fed up with sharing a room with me and my vomit and urine-soaked mattress.

And I looked at my relationships with girls. I had told so many of them that I loved them, asked so many to marry me. I was lying to fifteen girls, just so that we could have sex and I could have friends around me. I had a love deficiency syndrome. If a girl told me she loved me, I would be happy for a time. I was compensating for the love I had lost but causing so much pain along the way. It did not occur to me that I was behaving exactly like my father.

Finally, a girl named Lillian got up and spoke:

"Remember that God loves you unconditionally. Remember that His love for you does not depend on what you do, that He can be your source of self-worth and significance. And this same God who loves you also forgives you for every sin you have committed. But you must also know this: This God commands you to forgive every person who has hurt you, to forgive every person who has destroyed your self-esteem, to forgive every person who has crushed your self-worth. God commands you to forgive them, because if you do not you cannot truly be forgiven. You need to know that unforgiveness is the single most popular poison the Enemy uses against God's people. It causes everything from mental depression to health problems such as cancer and arthritis. Unforgiveness can open us up to curses, but when we forgive we are opened up to God's forgiveness. Forgiveness puts us in a receiving position when we pray, and it helps us become spiritually fruitful. When we keep God's commandments and love one another we prove that we love Jesus, and we abide in Christ's love. What a magnificent blessing forgiveness really is! God loves you; He forgives you and commands you to forgive others unconditionally."

My sense of calm and peace was torn down at once. Savage dogs within my soul ripped at the thawing heart, destroying in a flash of fur and teeth and blood the sense of hope that had begun to entice me. I was nothing but anger, nothing but rage, nothing but pain. How could she say those words? How could she tell me to forgive? It was volcanic, this anger; twenty years of it. I stood in the hall and screamed with all the rage and force and pain I could find: "I will never forgive my father, even if he walks on water!"

I ran out of the hall. I thought the gang would follow me, but they did not. Instead I heard later that some of them went up to the front for the altar call. Something was struggling within me, strangling me, choking me—the anger and bitterness, the demons of hatred and vengeance. I have never experienced such anger as I did then. I could not cope with the enormity of it. I thought that I would die.

My mother was so special to me that she was the only source of healing I knew I could rely on. I wanted to go back home to her, to sit on the dirt and have my tears turn into mud while she held me. I wanted to go back to her, even though I had treated her with such contempt.

Chapter Eight

Do You Believe in Me?

The roots of the East African Revival go back much further than September 1929. Yes, it is true that was the month when British missionary Joe Church sat on a hill in Kampala to pray and read the Bible for two days with his friend Simeoni Nsibambi. Yes, they felt a profound sense of God clearly identifying the problem at the heart of the African church—too little personal holiness among the members. And, yes, so many of us trace the revival that followed back to these forty-eight hours.

Yet the roots go back further. They go back to Cambridge University, from where Joe Church, as a student, became a Christian and was propelled south. They also reach back in history, four decades to be precise, to the time when D. L. Moody spoke at the university and helped ignite a passion for global missions that transformed the planet. Moody's story in turn has its own ancestral scribes; like a baton passed from runner to runner, revivals are incubated in the lives of the faithful from generation to generation.

All that being said, there are so many of us in Uganda, and throughout East Africa in general, whose lives have been changed as a result of 1929. It did not take long for things to happen, and after Joe Church returned to Gahini in Rwanda (my mother's hometown), Christians began to unite, to pray, and to confess their sins in public. Something was pulling them together, calling them on, urging them not to settle for a life of half-mumbled hymns and forgotten promises to God. They were hungry for more, and the tears that flowed were just one indication of the depth of their conviction.

As the repentance, prayers, and tears began to move out of the meetings and onto roads and hillsides, those who had no faith of their own began to take note. Many were converted, and soon the revival spread out from Rwanda to Burundi, Uganda, Kenya, and Tanzania. Lifestyles began to change as a result, and there was a marked drop in practices like polygamy and the branding of children with names that weighed on them like curses.

According to Michael Harper, a commentator writing in *Christian History* in 1986, the effects of the East African Revival have been more lasting than almost any other revival in history; it has impacted the majority of Protestant leaders in East Africa today.

Revival changed everything. It emphasized conviction of sin, judgment and righteousness, repentance, forgiveness, confession of sin, giving testimony, and restitution. It raised up brokenness, honesty, holiness, dedication, prayerfulness, expectancy, and every-member ministry. People gave generously, refocused on Scripture, and encouraged women in ministry. Integrity was a premium, and the church grew dramatically as a result.

Nevertheless, in some churches these foundations are being destroyed and revival has grown cold. People have worried more about the outward signs than the character that lies beneath them. Proverbs 22:28 says we should not uproot the landmarks that were planted by our forefathers. Unfortunately the church is in danger of uprooting these revival landmarks, and if this continues unchecked we shall lose our rights as the firstborn of this great revival. We are in danger of becoming much like Esau, who never received his birthright back even when he sought it in tears. We must pray for an unending revival. Here is a prayer I wrote, which has since become a song:

> Do it again, Lord, do it again,
> Send us the rains of revival again.
> Pour down the fire in the hills once again;
> Pour down the anointing again;
> Pour down conviction and repentance;
> Rebuild the broken walls again.
> Oh dig the wells again, Lord.

I have a personal interest in the legacy of the East African Revival because it touched my life, too, thanks to an old man named Mugyenzi, whom I was soon to meet on a bus. After I ran from the school and the choir and the words about forgiveness, I went into town to make the journey back home. Somehow I had enough money for the bus fare. While my head and hands raged at the idea of being told to forgive all those people who had inflicted such pain on me, I still knew this was not a time to fight. Previously, perhaps, I

would have stood and shouted at the choir, but not now. Something
had changed—only slightly, but enough for me to know that this
was not a battle ... this was a retreat. I needed to be back home.
Where else could I go with all this pain?

The bus was crowded, and I sat at the back. I do not remember
much of the first part of the journey, but as we reached the midpoint,
I started to panic. We were descending a steep hill, approaching a
part where the road met a river that slowed, broadened, and snaked
its way through trees with branches and leaves that trailed into the
waters. The location was loaded with meaning and memories for me.
Not only was this the river I had begged to swallow my life on the
day after Peninah's murder, but this very part where it bent around
on itself was the place where, just a year or two before, we had met
the hippo at night.

I was struggling to breathe. I needed to think clearly, to see through
the adrenaline. And it was then that a moment of clarity settled on me
and I knew, beyond all doubt, that if I crossed this bridge with such
bitterness and anger still unresolved and raging within me, I would
die. I do not know how I knew, but I felt this to be true to the core of
my being. If I did not change—and change right now—my life would
be damaged far beyond anything I had known already.

My heart told me that I had to say something, and as I got to
my feet I was almost hyperventilating. But I had to put words to this
sense that I wanted change in my heart. I needed to be a different
person by the time we had crossed the bridge.

I stood and spoke.

"From today I have agreed to forgive my father. I am not going
to kill him.

"And I am not going to kill my stepmothers ... or those who murdered my sister ... or those who raped my sisters."

I kept going, listing every one of the nineteen people on my list. I mentioned all their names and confessed other sins I had committed in my life—sins of sexual immorality, theft, witchcraft, lying, hatred ... on and on.

They thought I had finished, but then I added these words:

"From today I have accepted Jesus Christ. I am not going to kill anyone."

Then I fell to the floor, screaming, and wept bitterly.

Mugyenzi was on that bus. He was an old man—the sort you still see today, set too small within a suit made for a different man in a different time. Mugyenzi had grown up in Kabale and had been profoundly influenced by the East African Revival. I do not know how long he had been watching me, but as soon as I was on the floor he left his seat and came to crouch down next to me. He picked me up from the floor and held me in his arms. He addressed the rest of the passengers on the now stationary bus.

"What has hit this boy is nothing new. The same thing happened to me in 1936, and I confessed my sins in public, in tears just like this one here. I believe that he has accepted Jesus Christ today. Let us pray for him."

As he spoke I was feeling worse. It was as if something was trying to choke me, strangling me like my father throttled my mother. I could not breathe, could not inhale enough air to keep me alive. All I felt—all I *was*—was this mess of anger and death and hatred. I was filth. How could I even open my eyes, knowing that God knew all of this about me?

Mugyenzi prayed. His words were about forgiveness, love, and the cross. He prayed that I might know the truth about God's wild affection and grace for me.

As soon as Mugyenzi prayed I felt something leave me, replaced in turn by a peace that I had never experienced. I sat back on the seat and wept and wept and wept. But these were tears not of pain but of joy and peace—two feelings that were new and unfamiliar.

When the bus reached my home, Mugyenzi got off as well. We stood at the place where all this pain and sorrow had started—the tree beneath which I had been abandoned—but we did not stay there. We walked past that place, up the track and through the banana trees, to see my mother. It was a long walk, longer than I had ever remembered. I was concerned about what would happen next.

We crossed the stream, walked through the trees and up to our compound. My mother was standing there, having seen us approach some way off. I suppose she must have assumed that I was in trouble, that this man was escorting me from school, that I had been expelled for some shameful episode.

As soon as I saw her I broke down and wept uncontrollably. She did not know what was going on, and I could offer her no explanation. All I could say as I cried in her arms was, "Forgive me."

"It is all right," she repeated, over and over.

Eventually I found my words. "I am sorry. I have done so many terrible things to you. So many terrible things at school. But I wanted to say sorry because Jesus has forgiven me this morning."

Mugyenzi carried on from there, telling her about the bus and about my prayer. He and I had barely spoken up to this point. I had been in too much of a mess on the bus, and as we walked up to the compound our steps had been in silence. He wanted to know why I was trying to kill these nineteen people. I had not told him when we were on the bus, but as my mother told the whole story, he sat back and said, "I think you both need Jesus Christ. He is the only one who can sort out this family that is so broken."

He stayed with us for three hours. He began by telling me, "You must confess to your mother now. You must tell her everything."

So I did. Unlocked and unrestrained, I told her about every mistake I had made and kept hidden from her. I told her how I used to cheat her, exaggerating the school fees and pocketing the difference. I told her how I used to run away from school to go dancing, to fight, and to have sex with girls. I told her the hundred ways in which I had embarrassed her, how I had broken the vow I had made to her on that first walk to school.

I had been wondering about this moment from the time we got off the bus. How would she react? Surely she had no option other than to think badly of me. How would she respond to the news that I had behaved just as she must have feared I would?

And what about my change? She knew I wanted to join the army and kill all those people, and we had shared the lust for revenge. Would she allow me to break free from our murderous plan? How could I convince her that it was essential not only to let them live but to forgive them as well? And how would she cope with me telling people about my wayward life? She had made me promise not to embarrass her before—and I had broken that in my sin—but now I was about to do something that had a far greater potential to embarrass her. Would she agree? Would she give me her blessing? Was I about to lose the one parent who had truly loved me?

I was silent, and in the quiet Mugyenzi turned to my mother.

"What about you? You need to forgive your husband. Will you?"

The short answer is that, yes, she did. At that moment, in the midday sun, when just minutes before she had been carrying out her chores in the compound, the course of her life was utterly transformed. From where that change came from, I can point only to God. Only God could have given her the grace and the love to release her grip on a thirst for revenge that had been with her for years. Only God could make that change.

Mugyenzi was not finished.

"Your son has confessed to witchcraft," he said. "Where is it?"

My mother brought out the medicines from the house. She threw them on the fire. We both searched out every fetish we had bought from the witch doctors and added them to the flames. I went inside and brought out all the letters and photographs from girls I had been using. The fire consumed it all.

There was more to come from Mugyenzi.

He told me that because Jesus had forgiven me I would have to go and tell everyone what He had done. I needed to tell everyone I had hated and everyone I had hurt what I had done and how I had changed. He was like a madman, telling me to do all this. There was no sense that I should bask in the gentle love of my newfound faith for a few months. Mugyenzi, like all those other East African revivalists, knew that faith and lifestyle are intimately linked. If I did not change the way I lived, my love for Jesus would not outlast the year. Personal holiness was no accident; it was a discipline, put into action by a united head and heart. If I was serious, he said, I would not waste a moment.

He was right. I had every reason to keep this beautiful revelation of Jesus' love to myself. If I listened to the voices of caution, I would start to hold back, and for good reason. By confessing to my sins I was running a risk. Anyone who found out I had wanted to kill them had a case in the law courts against me. They could charge me with attempted murder or false accusation. I could have spent as many as fourteen years in jail for that. And the girls I was sleeping with—some were younger than me, some were married, some were even married to my cousins. Generally it was not illegal, but I was about to open myself up to people who had little love for me in the first place. With this news of my crimes they would have every reason to pursue their own revenge.

But no one who considered himself a born-again Christian would hold back on the public confession of sins. It was an essential part of faith, not an optional extra.

So I had to go and sort things out with people.

There was a lay preacher who lived nearby. I remember little about him other than that he had elephantiasis of the feet and so could not walk at all well. I also remember that he was a very dear man of God. Mugyenzi had stayed with us for three or four hours, and as he left he had encouraged us to go and tell someone we trusted in the village. My mother took me to this man's house to share our news. And there was also Deborah, my uncle's wife, who had told me so many stories from the Bible when I was a small boy. We told them both everything that had happened, words tumbling at first, then tears streaking all our faces. Some were of joy, but some of those tears were made heavy with sorrow.

After we had finished speaking they sang a song, "Tukutendereza Yesu." It was an old revival song that I am sure Mugyenzi would have known. I still sing it today:

Glory, glory to my Savior,
Glory, glory to the Lamb.
Oh! His precious blood has saved me,
Glory, glory to the Lamb.

I felt so confident, so good. To know that things were put right, that *I* had been put right—it was a dizzying, beautiful feeling. To sit among people who were kind and warm and full of love, and to hear them sing because of what we had just told them, to feel them hold us, to hear their prayers. It was as if I had been born into a different world.

Over the next three years, my five sisters became followers of Jesus. Our house transformed from a place of sorrow and witchcraft to a home cell, a church where day after day people would meet to pray. We went from being the cautionary tale of the surrounding area to being a light that shone bright with the love and healing power of Jesus. I praise God for that transforming power and still marvel at it today.

Forgiveness holds power that, I believe, we have barely begun to understand. The change in my life—as well as my mother's and sisters' lives—was dramatic and astounding, and it all came from God's forgiveness, from the cross, from the empty tomb, from the realization of sin and the desire to surrender to God. We can spend so much time and money talking and reading about the key to transformation—a diet, a makeover, a series of simple steps to turn life around—yet in truth it is found in the most famous death in all history. And while it is open and accessible to us all, none of us can fathom the mystery it contains.

That much was clear in the weeks and years to come. But there was more to be done right then. As well as confessing all to my mother and repeating the same with the preacher and Deborah, I knew I needed to present myself to each of the nineteen people I had intended to kill. It took me more than three years to see all of them. I began during the two weeks I was at home, visiting five people.

The first was one of my relatives. He lived close to our home, and within one or two days of my returning home, the lay preacher as well as others—including my mother—led me to his home. They spoke first.

"You must have heard the news about this boy."

Everyone had heard about me. I was the first teenager in the village to become a born-again Christian, and that was news in itself. This was the sort of thing reserved for uneducated people who never left the village. Even though I had been poor, the fact that I had managed to get to high school put me in a slightly different social grouping. I was not supposed to "find God" and change my life. I was supposed to complete school and feel superior to the uneducated masses.

I did not feel superior as I stood in front of my relative and his wife, looking at the dirt on the floor of their compound, wondering how this was going to be anything other than a disaster. It had been many years since I had been to this home, and my absence was the clearest sign that there was great hatred between us.

We stood, but he sat. His breathing was heavy, his eyes fixed on me. If my presence alone was enough to ignite his anger like this, what would happen when I started to confess my desire to put a bullet through his heart?

Deborah explained why we were here. She said that I wanted to put things right between us, to repair the damage that had been done. To do that, I had some things to say.

This was my cue to speak. What do you say to a man you wanted to kill? How do you start? I was mute for some seconds, unable to find even the first word. I looked at his wife, and his children, too, who were sitting quietly by the wall. How would they react to what I was about to say? His breathing was even sharper now, his eyes fueled by even more anger. What was he angry about? Did he know already what I was about to say? Was there some part of all of this that I was missing?

Eventually I spoke. I started with what I knew to be true.

"I want to tell you that yesterday I gave my life to Jesus Christ. One of the things that Jesus did in my life was to forgive me. I was angry and bitter about what happened to my sister, and Jesus forgave me. I was angry with you. People told me you were one of the ringleaders in that plot to kill her."

It was as if a switch had been flipped. His sharp breathing was no longer audible, and his eyes were pulled down from my own to the floor. I had accused him of a crime, and his reaction told me that I was right. Years—even days before—I would have rejoiced in this moment. The way I had planned it was similar: I would be standing; he would be seated. I would accuse him, and he would be flooded with guilt and shock. Then I would line up my gun, fire, and leave.

But that was before the choir and the bus and Mugyenzi and the flood of forgiveness from Jesus. Instead of basking in feelings of revenge, I knew I needed to submit to him. To this killer.

I spoke again.

"I had registered in the army so that I could kill you. But Jesus Christ arrested me, and I forgave you. I have come to tell you that I forgive you, and I have come to ask you to forgive me for being angry and bitter with you. I have never been here in your home since Peninah's death. I saw you as an enemy. I want to be your friend and relative again."

He was silent. Then, faint at first but growing stronger with every snatched breath, the weeping began. I do not know from whom it started, but it spread like a stream overwhelming a child's dam. It soaked into all of us there, him included.

Next to me was my mother, who was weeping more than the others. Perhaps she was remembering all the pain from the past. Incidents that I held in only a child's snatched recollection were far clearer for her, and the terror that must have propelled her out from Rwanda— the slaughter of her family by men with machetes held high—was just a fable to me. She had more pain than I had. Little wonder that her tears were heavier.

Within thirty minutes of our arriving at his house we had left. After I had confessed and asked for his forgiveness—and as the weeping was replaced with singing by some—his wife disappeared into the house and brought out some tea to drink and peanuts to eat. The significance of this act was enormous. It did not lie in the food or drink itself but in the act of hospitality. He did not say that he forgave me, but his wife's actions made a far bigger impression. I know that from the look of shock on his face as soon as she emerged with the heavy tray loaded with these symbols of unity.

Somebody prayed after we drank and ate, and then we left. That was all there was to it. It did not feel revolutionary, but I did know as I walked back to our home that I felt better. God had been with us, and the power of death was weaker. I had no idea that tea and peanuts held so much power.

Chapter Nine

Jesus Wept

It is only when you wake that you realize that what you considered to be normal within your dream was in fact quite unlike anything else in life. So it was with my first confession to one of my former targets: It was only as I walked away that I realized quite how terrified I had been. Eating together had been a practical act of restoration between us, and it was something we had not done for over five years. It meant they finally accepted us. This was wonderful, though I was still terrified.

The fear did not disappear quickly. It was there on Sunday as well, when I stood up at the front of the congregation at Kakiri-Kakiri Church of Uganda. This was the same church where I had hidden from the jigger hunters, the place where my faith had received its first morsels of nourishment and where my academic ability had been called out of its slumber. And here I was, standing in front of all these people who knew me, about to make myself vulnerable as a young man who had become a breeding ground for hatred, violence, immorality, and murder.

I decided not to mention any of the names of people I had wanted to kill but told the congregation about how Jesus had arrested me and breathed new life into me. I finished by saying, "Anyone here who I have had conflict with, I want you to know that I forgive you unconditionally. And I ask that you forgive me, too."

My stomach knotted as I stood and looked out at the people. Some were sitting on low benches; others were standing or leaning against the mud walls. Yet the nervous feeling I had then was nothing compared with what I felt about the next confession I would have to make. As I left the church I knew whom I must speak with. I might not have liked the idea, but I knew it was the next step to take on this journey.

In fact the man I visited next had no involvement in Peninah's murder. Our history was long, and I had wanted him dead for one hundred different reasons, all stored up within me over years of hatred and contempt. And then there had been an incident with a goat. Some years before—around the time when I was raging and drinking and fighting my internal civil war throughout the year after Peninah's death—I had killed his goat, albeit not intentionally. I had thrown a stone at it, and it had died. He was a bad man with a reputation for violence, and so at the time I had denied any involvement with the goat, and the police had arrested and beaten someone else as a result. But I think he always knew I was guilty.

God had reminded me of this incident and told me I needed to confess. I had avoided this man's house for years—as I had avoided other houses as well. There had been an enmity between our families that was toxic, and so it was important for me to go and sort this out.

I felt God say that this was something I should do alone, so I did. The man was drunk when I arrived at his home. I think this only increased his sense of surprise when he looked up and saw me. Sitting around the fire with him were his wife and his mother, and all three of them remained silent as I approached.

By now this was the fifth time I was going to tell my story, but I felt lost for words. I was stuck again. How should I start? I was not anticipating him being drunk, although on reflection there was nothing surprising about it. But it increased the fear. He was not a big man, but his yellowed eyes could flash with violence at the slightest provocation. I had seen him beat his children mercilessly, and within his reach were any number of weapons—a long stick, a machete, a log in the fire. Would he use any of these on me?

"My son," said his mother. She was old. Time and harsh conditions had not favored her beauty, but her words were the most beautiful you can ever hear: "I hear you have accepted Jesus as your Savior."

From that I told them everything. I told them about the way I had behaved, about the man I was becoming, and then about the choir and realization that without Jesus—and without forgiveness—I would be finished. And I told them about the goat. I told them I did not mean to do it, but it was I who had killed it. I told them that I thought about it every time I saw goats and that I was sorry and ready to pay any consequences.

The man looked at the fire. What was going on? Would he pull that stick out from his side and beat me? Would he tell me I would have to pay? Would he exact revenge in some other way?

It must have taken five minutes for the silence to be broken. It was his mother who broke it, singing a song about the woman who touched the hem of Jesus' garment: "Faith has made you well. Do not fear."

The man spoke up. "I knew you were the one who killed this goat. I knew it was you. And I was so angry."

He allowed the silence to return. He said nothing again, but this time there was no singing to fill the gaps. I could do nothing but wait.

Eventually he continued. "After five years that anger has died down. If God has forgiven you, who am I not to do the same?"

He was not a Christian at all, and he never even went along to church. To hear him talk of God with respect was surprising, but that feeling only increased as he confessed to me that he had also done things wrong. "Many things," he said. "Worse than killing a goat. Pray for us that we might be forgiven." So I did.

After a short prayer it was time to go. It was getting late, and it was already dark. The fire provided enough light for us in the compound, but beyond the fence it was going to be hard to see. I stood up to go.

"You cannot go alone," he said. "Let me escort you."

What could I say? I had no option other than to agree, and as soon as we left the compound it was clear he wanted me to walk in front while he followed behind. The path that wound across the valley was narrow, cut into the forest with just enough room for only one person to walk along at any time. These were the routes along which people carried their water or their matoke, arteries that were designed for commerce, not community.

He did not keep much distance between us. I could not feel him behind me, but I knew he was only one or two paces back. With every step I was convinced he was going to hit me, and my mind flooded with memories of the stories people told about this man—how his rage was such that he had even killed his own stepfather. My neck was exposed, and I feared that somewhere along the way he would reach into the darkness and pull out some weapon or other hidden for such a time as this. For two miles we walked in total silence. I had never felt such fear.

Eventually we both reached my home. When I knocked on the door, my mother opened up to see me and my companion standing just off behind me to the side.

She was shocked.

The man spoke up. "We have sorted ourselves out. You and my wife need to sort things out. And my mother."

And that was it. My mother agreed, and he disappeared. I was sighing with the sweetest relief at his first words—"We have sorted ourselves out"—and I knew he would not harm me now. Later my mother went and made her peace, and over the years the man and I developed a good friendship. I helped his daughter when she got married, and his son helped me build a home. Years later I helped lead his mother to Christ.

I saw others in those first two weeks as well. Gradually it did begin to get a little easier to start the confessions, but as my confidence grew so did the sense that there was one confession that stood out above all the others. This one had the very real potential to change everything in my life for the worse. Yet I knew that, after two weeks at home, it was time to go back to school.

I decided that as I returned to school I would have to take with me everything I had stolen from it. I had dinner plates, textbooks, clothes from other students. There was even a sickle that I had stolen from the headmaster's garden one day while I was working there. I had denied it so vehemently at the time, but now I was about to present him with overwhelming evidence that I had tricked him and treated him like a fool ever since I had arrived there.

All the headmaster knew was that I had run away two weeks ago. My return itself would be an issue, and I made straight for his office when I arrived. On his desk I placed the three boxes with the stolen items spilling out of them.

I told him what had happened—about the bus trip, the conversion, and the changes that were starting. This was easy. What followed next was not. I confessed to my part in the riot, to my drinking, my womanizing, my stealing, my lying, my violence, my hatred, my treating him like a fool. As I spoke he looked through the items on his desk: spoons, cups, plates. He saw the sickle and looked up at me. He did the same when he saw one of his son's footballs that had gone missing from the garden—both things I had denied all knowledge of in the past.

"Are you aware that if a thief is caught they are expelled?"

"Yes."

"Then go to the dormitory, and I will meet with the governors. Wait there until I send for you."

I walked down the hill to my dormitory. It had been just two weeks since I had left there, but I was immediately struck by how alien it felt. My mattress held the low, unrelenting smell of stale urine and vomit. How could I have lived like this? How could I have considered this any sort of life worth pursuing? I was alone in the dormitory—a room with one small window and eight other mattresses on the floor. So many times I had come in here looking to fight, only to end up collapsed and incontinent on my heap of old straw in the corner. I had been an animal. I wanted nothing more to do with that life, and if the governors decided that my crimes should be given even a fraction of the punishments they deserved, I would never be able to return. *This might well be the last time I lie here,* I thought.

What would I do? I had hoped that education might be my way out, that it might lead me into the army and then into the shoes of a killer. But now that I had been born again, I saw that education need not necessarily lead me to kill. If I could complete school, then I might be able to teach or become a minister. I might be able to do more for God and others. I might be able to do more than I had ever hoped. But that sort of talk was pointless. I was sure I was going to be expelled. I deserved nothing less.

I was pulled out of my thoughts by the sound of the school drum. It was only ever beaten if there was an emergency or if the headmaster desperately wanted everyone to gather. There was always danger in the air when the drum was beaten; either someone was going, some big man from the government was on his way, or something else was wrong. I am not sure I thought it was anything to do with me when the rhythm started up.

The school compound was set up so that there was an area where we could all gather in front of the school offices. There was a platform upon which the headmaster and visitors would stand and in front of which we could gather. The school site was set on the side of a hill, and the land had been terraced all the way down to make the best use of it. Down beneath the top level with the offices and meeting area were the classrooms. One more terrace down was the library, then below that the dormitories. As I climbed up, running up the hill with students pouring out of classrooms, I became lost in the crowd. As I approached the top I could see the platform; on it were all the boxes I had left in the headmaster's office.

We had a motto in school and it came into my mind at that point, blocking out all other thoughts: *The suspected thief is killed.* I knew it was over for me. All the violence I had handed out was about to come back to me.

The headmaster waited for the students to assemble, and then he spoke. He looked directly at me.

"Zinomuhangi, come here."

It was the name my father had given me, the one that meant "they have a creator." I would have preferred it if he had called me by the other name my father had given me—Barisigara ("the one who will stay"), but that was hoping for too much from the man whose trust and kindness I had treated with such contempt.

"We have called you because we have a very urgent matter. We have arrested a thief who has been stealing from all of us. Open these boxes, Zinomuhangi."

The rest of the school had no idea that I was the accused; they just thought I was helping. I carefully laid out every item on the platform. With each piece I handled I saw the evidence against me mounting. I knew my guilt already, but as each item passed from box to hand to platform, I was reminded again of my sins. Why had I stolen so much? Why had I been so greedy, so wrong? Why had I lived like this?

The rest of the boys started whistling. They started calling out, "Where is the bird? Where is the bird?" It was the word we always used to describe a thief, and they shouted nonstop … *a bird, a bird, a bird.*

They could not be stopped.

The only thing I had on my side was the gang. They were all there. Perhaps they would help me. But what could they do? They knew nothing other than the violence I had embraced so fully before all of this.

Once all the items were on the platform, the headmaster looked at me. He said nothing. The shouts from the crowd died down as they, too, followed his gaze. It was my turn to speak.

I told them everything. I did not start with the events of two weeks before but went all the way back to my childhood. I told them about my father, about the abuse at the hands of my sister, about my uncle and the machete and the humiliations in front of the whole village. I told them about Peninah and wanting to kill myself and about the waterfall and Aidah Mary. I told them about the list, the gang, and the army. And I told them about the items I had taken out of the box—how I had stolen them all. I stood there in front of eight hundred students and told them everything. I declared that I was leaving the gang as of that moment. I denounced fighting, drinking, and treating girls so badly.

My words built up to a crescendo as I was my own prosecution. This was not a debate but a trial—a trial without defense. I had no defense; I had nothing to say to try to play down the pain I had caused or the wrong I had done. I exhaled my final words.

"I know a thief is to pay for his sins, and I am ready to pay."

I stopped.

The headmaster had never heard my story in full. My mother had told him much of it, but there were parts she had skipped over. In front of the school I had held nothing back. The headmaster was in tears. The students looked on in shock. None of them knew the truth about me. I had tried to convince the rest of my gang mates that I was rich, but this speech undid all I had told them before. The gang leader was not impressed, and to taunt me he started singing the chorus of "Tukutendereza Yesu." Most of the eight hundred students sang in unison and made fun of me, the thief who stood in front of them. But to me the name of the Lord had been glorified, even by the Muslim students in the crowd. Their singing made my shaking legs stand firm.

The headmaster spoke first. "If God could arrest everyone who has committed a crime here, there would not be many of us left. I am going to talk to the board of governors and see what can be done."

And that was it. The students were told to go back to classes and I was expected to do the same. There was no judgment, no beating, but no full reprieve either. I walked down the hill in the crowd, boys talking to me, asking me if it was all true, if I really had done all those things. I do not remember what my answers were. It was my turn to be in shock.

A week later the headmaster told me of the decision of the governors. They had agreed to forgive me. The drum beat again, and the school was assembled and told the news. They were told how I was also appointed school librarian because the governors guessed I would have a good idea how students were stealing books. As a matter of fact I did, and from that moment on I was one of the best librarians the school had ever had. Not many books went missing on my watch.

I also joined the school's Scripture Union group and learned how to read the Bible, how to pray, and how to preach. They asked me to join them in traveling to other schools and to give my testimony. I discovered that, far from being filled with gang members and nothing else, the school was alive with wonderful Christians. Other students took me alongside them, including the son of Mugyenzi, the man I had met on the bus and who had brought such healing to me and my mother on that morning. These students did an incredible work and taught me a lot. They looked out for me, protected me, and nurtured me.

As well as Scripture Union, Campus Crusade for Christ was so gifted at teaching me how to grow as a Christian and how to carry out person-to-person evangelism using the four spiritual laws, things I still find helpful even today. I had never paid it much attention before, but there was a cathedral opposite the school. Lots of the old revivalists would meet there, and I made a habit of spending time with them. They taught us how to repent, how to spot the characteristics of revival, and what part personal holiness played in it all. It was a big movement, and we were united. Slowly but steadily I started to preach.

A little while later, as my life began to settle into its new rhythm, I was at home and knew the time was right to talk to the woman who had fed the killers and shown them to Peninah's house, waiting to hear the shots fired before turning around and returning home. To talk to her about all of this was a painful task, made more painful by the history between us. Before Peninah's murder this woman was my favorite. When I was small she had fed me many times, and I had always liked her more than the other women around. After Peninah's murder she used to come to visit us, to try to cover up her guilt and pretend that all was well between us, but we always disliked her.

It was painful to sit down and talk to her. And it was difficult as well. I had tried on one or two earlier occasions, but it had never worked. She did not want to discuss it and would always pretend she did not know what I was talking about.

But this time, somehow, I knew it was right. Instead of talking about me, I started with the truth about her: "I heard you were in the group of people who murdered Peninah. So I have come to sort things out with you."

All that happened was this: She cried. And cried. And cried. The tears threatened never to cease. In time, though, as they eased off, she said, "I do not know whether God will ever forgive me. But I want peace with you, my son. I want peace."

And that is what followed between us. Our reconciliation became one of the most treasured changes in my new life. It did not stop there, either. She became a born-again Christian. Almost twenty years later, I still love to tell the story of how it happened.

Many years later, she got sick. She was admitted into Kisiizi Hospital—the one at the bottom of the waterfall, so close that you can hear the roar as you stand in the compound and almost feel the spray. The hospital was running a mission at the time, and they invited many preachers to come in and speak to the staff and patients. They asked me to join them and give my testimony.

They say that white people teach, while Africans preach. I do not know about that—I have some good *muzungu* friends who preach the Word with passion and zeal. But I also know that if you invite me up to the front of your church to say a few words, I will probably speak for a little longer than you might expect. We say that *muzungu* have the watch but we Africans have the time. This is what happened on the Friday night of the mission in Kisiizi Hospital. I was invited to give my testimony but ended up preaching. There were loudspeakers throughout the hospital, and I know she was listening as I told my story and gave the gospel message. Included in my testimony were a few words about the reconciliation with her. I did not mention her by name, but she knew I was talking about her.

The next day there was another meeting, and I went along. I was surprised to see that she had left her bed and was sitting upstairs on the veranda of the hospital ward. It may not have appeared all that significant to an observer, but to me—as well as her daughter, who was also a born-again Christian—her shift away from her bed to the outside, where she could hear and see the preachers more clearly, was deeply symbolic and profoundly encouraging. Her daughter and I felt inspired to pray for her with even greater determination.

On Sunday another man was preaching, and he spoke well. After speaking he said, "Today there are some people God has been speaking to. God brought you to this hospital not to get physical healing but spiritual healing. I want you to come here, and we will pray for you, and you will get physically and spiritually healed. If you want this, come up to stand with me."

She was in the hospital receiving treatment for various conditions—high blood pressure, severe arthritis, and so on. I watched the cluster of people approach the preacher, who was standing in front of a makeshift altar, and at first did not notice her shuffling up with her two walking sticks guiding her steps.

As she reached the front she threw down both walking sticks. Her hands held aloft, she turned around to face the congregation. Her face was transformed. Gone was the burden of guilt and the lines of pain. She simply shone. I jumped up, ran to her, hugged her, and we both cried for what must have been ten minutes.

Eventually she was given the microphone: "I thank God today. He has healed me physically and spiritually, and today I want to give my life to Christ."

She was no stranger to Christianity, but her past made her words even more dramatic. Formerly, her husband was a church leader. Because of the problems that had taken root and thrived amid their hatred and anger, he had stopped being a lay preacher and taken a swift descent to becoming a drunkard. He remained as such even after her conversion, but she became an even more significant member of our family. She has done a great deal to bring many of them to Jesus Christ. Now she visits me when she comes to Kampala, she calls me when she is sick, and we have become great, great friends. I want to thank God so much for that.

It has not been easy to reach this point. Even after that weekend in the hospital—for years afterward, in fact—I would often remember her and feel the same old feelings of hatred and anger toward her. I reached a stage where I put her photo in my Bible so that when those old feelings of resentment came to me, I could look at her and forgive her. It was a tool that really helped me, and within three years we were much better.

Within weeks of my becoming a Christian, I could see that God was teaching me about forgiveness. While my own confession and absolution had taken only a matter of hours, the issue of how to forgive others was taught over a far, far longer period of time. Instead of hours, I have spent decades learning why I need to forgive. Through it God has taught me that restoring broken relationships is a vital part of following Jesus. Even as a growing Christian these lessons were so valuable to me.

Today I am no expert on the matter. Instead of a professor I am like a schoolboy with a soccer ball made out of tape, plastic bags, and rags. I am fascinated by forgiveness, drawn to it, compelled by it, and delighted when anyone wants to join me. That is what revolutionary forgiveness becomes after a while—a passion. It draws us in, yet it does not overrule us. We must still make the choice to overcome our reservations.

Back then I still had so many reservations. I may have spoken with many of the people on my list, but there was one more restoration ahead that would cost me far more than the others. One of my aunt's daughters brought this to my attention just a few weeks after her mother's conversion.

"What about your father? Surely your forgiveness must extend to him, eh, Birungi?"

This daughter I was speaking with was dying of HIV/AIDS. I was meeting with her to pray, and the news of her mother's transformation had left an indelible mark of peace and happiness on her emaciated frame. For many, many years she had prayed for her mother, longing that she, too, would know the power of Jesus' love, acceptance, and forgiveness. Now, when she was just a few weeks away from death, her prayer had been answered.

In those few months between the dawn of her mother's new life and the nightfall of her own we often talked and prayed. Before her body lost its battle against relentless infection, she asked me, If God had transformed her mother's life so dramatically, then why could I not expect Him to do the same for my father?

I knew she was right. But that did not make me any less terrified.

Chapter Ten

Take Away the Stone

My father's transformation was a miracle. I did not believe he would ever change. But if God had changed others dramatically, there was a chance the same power could also transform my father.

How do you encourage transformation? We know we are powerless to create and sustain it ourselves, but do we have a part to play in creating the environment in which true revolutionary change can take place? I think we do. I think we can act as midwife to the miraculous transformation God instigates. I think we can play our part and roll away the stone, just as Lazarus's friends did. And all of this, I believe, starts with prayer.

And so, hungry for change in our father's life, we started a prayer movement. For months we prayed, my family and I, pleading with God to break through and change his heart. We prayed for healing, for restoration, for deliverance. We spent many hours in silence and many more in tears. Eventually, after two years, came the first sign that God was clearly at work; we received news that our father was sick.

We did not know it at the time, but he had been abandoned by his wives. He had cancer and was unable to work. His finances had sprung a leak, and his wives had followed the exodus. Yet he was not alone. When he first settled in the area, he had encouraged so many families from our village to migrate with him—coming back and tempting them with huge sweet potatoes. Many of them who had joined him still had connections back in the old village. News of what had happened to his first wife and her children—the ones he had turned his back on—had reached my father's friends.

One of them told him, "Your children are doing well. Something has changed in them. Why don't you try to get in touch with them to see if they might be able to help you?"

So my father put a series of announcements on the radio. There were seven of them in all, repeating the same message: "I am terribly sick, in a very critical condition. Please, my children, come and take me to the hospital."

He was frustrated at having to do this, but he called for our help despite the humiliation. People in our village heard the broadcast and told us about it. It left us in an awkward situation; we had prayed so long for restoration, but to hear that he was "in a critical condition" was not something we had anticipated. Although we had spent two years praying for change, we had spent two decades before that longing for news of his death. We met at home to talk about it, and at first the general feeling was that he deserved to die. We slipped back into the old way of things, and most of us felt that we should let him die. After all, he had rejected us. At first I felt that way. But not for long.

In time I remembered the words of Jesus on the cross: "Father, forgive them, for they do not know what they are doing."

I knew we had to help, so my sisters, my mother, and I talked. We would never have another father again. This man, Boniface, was our only one, despite all the pain and shame he had handed out to us. We had prayed for transformation, so was this not God giving us an opportunity to meet with him, to help him, and possibly to be reconciled? Why could we not try?

My mother had some money, so we hired a car to drive us to see him. I had not seen him for many years—more than ten. I had been a teenager when we had last met, a year before Peninah was murdered. He had made two trips back to the village after he had abandoned us, and neither of them had gone well. He was there simply to recruit more people to move with him to Queen Elizabeth National Park, and on the first trip he would come back to our house only at night, when he was drunk. We did not fight him, and we did not talk. He forced himself on my mother when he returned home, leaving her pregnant on both occasions.

Cancer had changed him. Or perhaps it was that he, too, had tasted the bitterness of abandonment now that his wives had gone. He looked ill and weak, but there was something else about him; he was *less* than he used to be. Perhaps it was because I was larger now, but he seemed so small that I wondered how such a man had ever caused us such devastation.

We did not talk. He was too ill for conversation, as the cancer had spread throughout his intestines, leaving him almost in a coma. At this stage we were not there for reconciliation, merely rescue. We brought him back to the village, but not to our home. We took him to the hospital at Kisiizi, the same place where I had tried to commit suicide on the waterfalls, and the same hospital where my aunt had met with God dramatically. Perhaps the same thing would happen for him?

The doctors removed large parts of his intestines, and he gradually started to improve. I had no idea what was going on; was this God's plan? Things were changing so slowly that it was hard to know what to do. My mother knew, though. She was good to him, kinder, I think, than any person I have ever witnessed. She fed him, nursed him, bathed him, and offered all sorts of acts of mercy despite what he did when he rejected, abandoned, and cursed her to be blown away like dust. My sisters and brothers—whom he had also rejected, cursed, abandoned, and disowned—would walk the ten miles every day from home to the hospital to bring him food despite the wicked things he did to us. The reconciliation between my father and mother took place over these months, through meals and kindness and sacrifice.

In time he was stronger and was told he would be discharged from the hospital. Today it is clear that his period of recovery after the surgery was vital for our renewal as well. We grew accustomed to the idea of having him around, and we got used to the idea that he was someone to whom we should show kindness. We found ourselves in the habit of believing we had a father again.

All that slow restoration came to fulfillment on the day he left the hospital and returned home with us. It was the greatest day in my life. I never thought our father would ever come back and settle at home. But he did, and that moment started when he stepped out of the car—with my mother—at the tree by the main road where he had abandoned us.

I do not know what he was thinking at that moment. Did he remember the day when he beat us, tipped out that bucket of ash, and cursed us? I do not know. Perhaps he did not remember that day at all. It does not matter really, for what followed when he eventually arrived at our house was as clear a sign as we could ever have wished for that he was sorry for what had happened.

We were all waiting at home to greet him. But the journey was not yet over. We had gathered for his arrival, none of us with any idea of how things would progress. As his undersized frame appeared in the doorway, some of my sisters screamed. And then there were the tears. For twenty minutes we cried, every one of us. I had never seen an old man crying—never—but my father wept like a child. Breath escaped him, and, like the psalmist said, his tears were his only food.

My mind was full of questions about these tears. What were they—tears of sorrow, of fear, of pain? I knew he was stronger than when we had taken him to the hospital, but was he able to cope with this experience? Would all this prove to be too much for his refugee body?

Eventually, fittingly, it was my father who broke the silence. In a voice every bit as fragile as his physique, he spoke softly.

"My children, please, I want you to forgive me. I brought pain to you. I rejected you. I abandoned you. I never knew that you would be the ones to save my life."

Then he said a proverb in our local language:

"A fool hates somebody who loves him."

We were sitting in the main room of my mother's house, with a low table in the middle and chairs all around. He sat on one side, while my sisters, brothers, and I were opposite. After he recited the proverb he stood up and moved from his side over to us. He stood in front of Peace, my elder sister, who looks so beautiful, so much like my mother. She was the one who was abducted and defiled at a young age and forced to marry a man who continues to mistreat her to this day.

My father had always treated her with contempt. None of us ever knew why, but it was clear he thought even less of her than he did the rest of us.

"My daughter," he said, "even from the moment you were born, I never liked you. Please forgive me."

They hugged, and gradually, one by one, we started to talk. We confessed the things we had hated him for. We told him the truth, holding nothing back. We talked about feeling like we were enemies, about wishing him dead. He spoke of the humiliation of our beating him, of the way he and his wives celebrated when they heard that Peninah had been murdered. He did not know why, but his hatred of us had been so great that his own daughter's murder sparked joy. Their plan had been to cripple us financially, to make us social misfits, so Peninah's death was cause for celebration, even though he was clear that he had nothing to do with it.

People started to come to our house, to see Boniface back with his first wife and children. They came and saw us forgive each other, saw us crying tears of joy, holding on to each other without fear of violence.

And we waited to see whether he had really changed.

He started coming home early, not drunk either. We started eating together, and he and my mother worked in the garden together, went to the market together, went to church together. In just a few weeks we started to regain our self-esteem as children. Finally we had someone we could call father. It is hard to find the words to quite describe what a difference that made to us.

The change started to affect more than my mother, sisters, brothers, and me. My father went to apologize to Eric, Peninah's husband, for not coming to help bury her. Then he brought some of the relatives with whom we had had misunderstandings for many years. These were the people who had been complicit in his crimes, the ones who had taken his side. He brought along to our house his sisters who had spent so many years defending their brother. These were the relatives who had hurt, embarrassed, and humiliated us terribly. He made a big step, calling his relatives to our home and trying to be an instrument of peace.

In those days people in the village ate communally, and it was not uncommon for folk to arrive with food to share with our father, mother, and us. They would come, we would eat, and we would talk over the issues, going back over all the past hurts and putting them right. We fed on food and forgiveness, and it made us stronger.

For two or three years we had a great time with him. He talked to us and went to church with us; he went to weddings together with our mother. That was their honeymoon.

All along I have spoken about my sisters, but I have not told you so very much about my brothers. I had three—James, Robert, and Fred—although two of them are not alive today. Robert and James were born before our father abandoned us and are no longer living, while Fred, who is a twin with Jennifer, is still alive. He and Jennifer are the last born in our family and were conceived during my father's second return after our abandonment.

I remember the first time my father returned to us. It was five years since he had left us weeping by the side of the road. He had come back to recruit more people to move with him to his new home. He was ashamed of coming to our house and first stayed at my uncle's place, fearing the taboos that say that after abandoning your home and vowing never to return, you will die if you go back. He first took traditional medicine before he entered our house and then spent five days with us.

Those days were not good days. We did not talk to him. We would go to school very early in the morning and leave him in bed. At night he would come home late and drunk. I wonder how my mother slept with him with the hatred in her heart, but because of cultural laws she could not lock him out. She had also taken traditional cleansing medicine, so I suppose she felt in some way protected.

She got pregnant in those five days and later gave birth to Grace Ankunda, whose name means "God loves me." My father left, having convinced four families to move with him.

Four years later he returned, looking for more people to join him. This time he stayed for twelve days, again leaving my mother pregnant—this time with the twins, Fred and Jennifer.

Our father had always rejected Fred, Grace, and Jennifer. My mother had been clear that he was their father, but many people believed him when he said he was not. He accused her of infidelity, but the timing was such that they really only could have been his. As my mother said, why would she become sexually immoral when he was around? Would she not have done it while he was away?

These children grew up in a poisonous environment. People in the village told them that their father was the lay preacher, a good man who had stood by us through thick and thin. The rumors wounded Fred, Grace, and Jennifer, and they grew to be consumed by bitterness. They were greatly traumatized by the slander, and my mother was humiliated. They had been doubly abandoned—by their father and by their village.

One of the greatest acts of my father was his public acceptance of these children as his own. It solved so many problems that had divided the family and scarred three innocent young children so deeply.

My father's return brought so much healing, but it did not change things for us financially. He was bankrupt, and we were the ones who had to look after him. His illness had drained the last of his resources, as an earlier tragedy had used up so much of his money. He had lost a child while living in Queen Elizabeth National Park. His little boy was just five years old when my father stepped out of the compound to check on his cows. When he came back the little boy was gone. The boy had been alone for only a quarter of an hour, but that had been enough time for him to disappear. Living in the national park meant there were wild animals around. My father and his wife Lodah went to see many witch doctors in an attempt to find their missing son and in the process spent so much money that they had to sell most of their cattle and goats. The loss of this son crippled the family, as the witch doctors continued to hold out the prospect of a safe return, if only the anxious parents would spend just a little more money and a few more animals.

According to the witch doctors the boy had not been taken by an animal. They thought he had been bewitched by my mother. We heard this at the time, and it worried my mother greatly, so much so that she, too, visited a witch doctor to get protection against any possible attacks from her husband. There was so much fear going around that it was hard to know what was true.

Witchcraft remains a severe problem in Uganda today. People often sacrifice animals, but some demons demand bigger sacrifices … human ones. People believe that when you sacrifice a human you appease the gods. That is why they thought my mother sacrificed that boy to protect her own children. She did not, but it is true that whenever we heard their threats, we would go to more witch doctors to protect ourselves, too.

Child sacrifice is a horrendous reality for us today. Many will try to keep it hidden, but we all know it takes place. Some people believe that if you cut off a child's head their blood will seal whatever covenant you make. They believe that if you put a child's head or body in the foundations of a house, the building will stand longer. There are newspaper stories about these things, claiming that in the last two years as many as nine hundred children have been sacrificed, while over one hundred have been trafficked out of Uganda to Sudan, Congo, and other countries.

The sad thing is that there is no political will to change it, and so child trafficking becomes an even more lucrative criminal enterprise. Our leader, Museveni, has made it easier for these things to happen. He has opened up freedom of worship, so that in Uganda now it is no longer Christianity that matters most; all traditional African religions share equal status. Animism, sorcery, and witchcraft are a growing national problem. The Chinese have poured a lot of money into research of traditional medicine, and that has led to the creation of the Traditional Healers and Herbalists Association, making it hard to differentiate between an herbalist and a witch doctor. The trade in human body parts—from female breasts to genitalia—is increasing. One recent story told of a man who was arrested on the way to a witch doctor who was going to buy and then sacrifice the man's twin children for 100 million Ugandan shillings—a little over forty thousand dollars.

In Uganda we have only one medical doctor for every seven thousand people, yet we have one witch doctor for every two thousand people. We are one of the centers for witchcraft, but we are not alone. Most African people believe in witchcraft and sorcery rather than in the healing that comes from Christ. Their first thought when illness strikes is to contact a witch doctor. And, in many ways, witch doctors work. But just like Satan appearing to Jesus in the wilderness, their power is built on nothing but destruction and death. The church must find its voice on this issue, and we must rediscover the ministry of healing and deliverance to counter all this evil.

My father denounced witchcraft when he came home. But the boy never did come back.

Of all the changes, the fact that my father started to talk about us positively was one of the most welcome. For many years every word from him about us had been negative, but now he started to talk positively about our mother, about my sisters and my brothers and me. People would come up and say to me, "Hey, Birungi, your father said you are a good boy."

That made a great impact on the village and a great impact on us. We were chronically negative, and yet he started to plant the spirit of positivism. He would even tell men who had openly despised us that we had saved his life, and in time he became a leading example of talking about your wife and children positively.

After two years he did something profound. He told our mother, "I believe that God is doing something great. I am going back to Queen Elizabeth National Park in Bunyaruguru to bring my other wives back here."

My mother was not as opposed to this as you might think. She knew—as we all did—that full restoration was needed, and the toxic relationships with the other wives could only be dealt with face-to-face.

He brought two of them back, Lodah and Kobucence. Lodah was the mother of the boy who had gone missing. She was the most expensive of all his brides, costing four cows and twelve goats. She was very beautiful as well as expensive, but I never liked her as much as the day she returned home to us and we all apologized to one another. Kobucence was the youngest wife and the favorite. We ate together, and the reconciliation was complete.

The wives went back after we all agreed that the children needed to get to know each other. So my father arranged a family meeting. We all contributed some money by selling crops or something similar and we all came together: thirty children, twenty-seven grandchildren, five of his wives. We had bought a cow from my sister Winnie and slaughtered it. The reconciliation party included all our aunts and uncles—there were over eighty people gathered—and in front of them all, my father gave a speech.

He described how we had hated one another, how we had used witch doctors against one another, and how God had brought reconciliation to us all. He said that because I had been a channel of healing and reconciliation, he would be happy to leave his family in my hands. He made me his heir that day, in front of all those people.

It was a very important moment, to know that when he died I would take on the family.

We had been such terrible enemies at the start, and perhaps he had sinned against me more than he had against the others, rejecting me as his first son and heir, leaving me with the responsibility of caring for my family but no tools with which to support them. I was so very happy about being his heir that I still give thanks to God for it even today. And when my father died, all the members of the family—wives, children, grandchildren—chose to respect me. Perhaps my father chose me because I chose to forgive, or perhaps he chose me because he thought I would do the job the best. I do not know. But I am sure of this: Forgiveness transforms every one of us from outcast to heir.

≋

Not that everything always went the way I had hoped. I was still working through my list of people I had wanted to kill, and my father helped me approach some of the families. One conversation did not go well.

John was an uncle of mine. I approached him with my father. John was furious when he saw us, and it only got worse when I told him I had wanted him dead for the part he played in Peninah's murder. He shouted that we were falsely accusing him and that we were poisoning people against him. He told us to never again step foot in his compound.

For many years we did not talk. But after five years I had a reason to break the silence. I knew he was unwell, so I went back to pray for him. He was suffering from malaria, but according to his wife he was suffering from demonic attack—he was a traditionalist, and they claimed he had not pleased his gods, who were now unhappy. But I prayed for him, talked to him, and led him in the sinner's prayer, and he accepted Jesus as his Savior. He died years later, still a Christian, with his wife sharing his faith. For a time I was able to pay school fees for his grandchildren, and one of them stayed with my wife and me in Kampala.

We knew John had sold a cow in order to contribute money to Peninah's murder, and having his grandson Livingstone stay with us was a clear and constant reminder of the pain that had been caused and the change that had taken place.

The final person with whom I had to set things right was Eric's first wife, the co-wife of Peninah. It was not until 1997 that this happened, eighteen years after Peninah's murder, and there was a reason it took so long. This woman had been the instigator of the murder, and Eric had chased her away once the truth had come out. For many years we had prayed about it, looking for opportunities to be reconciled with her, but for so much of the time it seemed impossible. There were times when I feared for my life; she had brothers who knew about the conflict between us, and it was all very difficult.

One day I met her quite by accident. I was sent on mission by the diocese, and their home church was one of the ones under my jurisdiction. I gave my testimony, explaining how I had been able to forgive and sharing how I did not have anybody in my heart whom I hated.

She was seated in the congregation. Eric had died of a heart attack, and she had returned to Kantare to attend his funeral. At the end of the service I stood in the doorway, greeting people as they left. She stood in front of me. I said hello. She did not look the way I remembered her; memory had turned her into a bitter-looking monster, but she was friendlier, calm, and less tense than I thought she would be. Yet we still had no time to talk.

Her sons decided to bring her back to her home near the house where I had last seen Peninah's body, where Eric's third wife, Peace, now lived. We all gathered there: Eric's first wife, her sons, Peace, and my aunt Jane. There was one other person there as well—my niece Katy, the one whom as a baby I had removed from her mother's lifeless, blood-soaked breast.

My mother had warned me not to eat any food that was offered—for fear of being poisoned—but as I sat there, this woman I had feared and hated in equal measure for so long broke down.

"I am sorry I killed your sister," she said. "She destroyed my home, my marriage, my business. She was younger and Eric favored her and I had lost everything to her. Out of anger and jealousy I decided she did not deserve to be happy."

She told me she knew that people thought of her as a killer and that she needed to give her life to God. I got the chance to express my forgiveness to her verbally and physically, in front of my aunt. But I was wondering how Katy felt. She cried as she heard this woman—who had so strenuously denied any involvement in her mother's death for so long—finally confess to the truth.

After a year the woman became sick and died and was buried in the same garden as Peninah. And so both of Eric's first two wives died as born-again Christians.

As so many of my family became Christians, there was great change in the village. So many people had been involved in this story of hatred and abuse, murder and denial, that when God rolled away our stone there was a sort of holy chaos that followed.

I talk a lot about revolutionary forgiveness because that is the best way I can think of to describe what happened to me. A revolution is a fundamental change that turns things upside down, something that affects not just individuals but also the wider community. Today in my home region, there are clear signs that things have changed. Domestic violence, especially against children, has decreased. The place is full of living testimonies, walking symbols of the power of forgiveness. Many, many teenagers have been completely transformed; they know that tough times come and go but that they can stand and be somebody. They see that Christianity has something to do with changing people's lives for the better. They expect to make a difference, not just carry on as before except with a slightly better record of church attendance. They are hungry for change and look to God to instigate it.

In my life and ministry, I have seen so many people in spiritual bondage due to bitterness, blame, and unforgiveness. It is not uncommon to find people harassed by demons because of bitterness in their hearts. After all, bitterness is also known in the Bible as spiritual poison: "For I perceive that thou art in the gall [poison] of bitterness, and in the bond of iniquity" (Acts 8:23).

Unforgiveness not only gives demons the right or ability to torment us, but it also prevents God from forgiving our own sins. Now this is serious, for if we cry out for God's help with unforgiveness in our hearts, He looks down and sees our sins before Him. Unforgiveness puts up a wall in our relationship with our heavenly Father. Jesus was very clear that if we are to be forgiven, we cannot be unforgiving toward others: "But if ye forgive not men their tres-passes, neither will your Father forgive your trespasses" (Matt. 6:15).

We need to give to God the things that belong to Him. Unforgiveness is actually removing something that belongs to God and taking matters into our own hands. God's Word tells us clearly that we should allow God to bring His wrath upon that person and let Him have the room to repay those who wrong us. Romans 12:19 says, "Dearly beloved, avenge not yourselves, but rather give place unto wrath: for it is written, Vengeance is mine; I will repay, saith the Lord."

Those who have wronged us will reap what they sow. If you choose to forgive somebody, he may be off your hook, but that does not mean he is off God's. God's Word tells us clearly that what we sow we shall reap: "Be not deceived; God is not mocked: for whatsoever a man soweth, that shall he also reap" (Gal. 6:7).

Unforgiveness is actually a form of hate against another person. If a person hates somebody, it is a sign that the person lacks love in his heart. Why? He is not firmly rooted and grounded in the love of Christ, and Christ's love is not flowing through him. As simple as that sounds, that is how it works. What somebody may have done against us is one thing, but if you take Satan's bait of unforgiveness to heart, it will do much more harm than that person did. Do you want to continue to allow someone else's mess to trouble you even more? Has there not been enough damage? Allowing yourself to hang on to hard feelings and become bitter only causes your wound to become even more infected spiritually. Honestly ask yourself, what good is it doing you to hold on to the hurt and bitterness that the Enemy has tried to plant within you? It is doing nothing but harm and is holding you in bondage spiritually. The only reason you are holding on to those feelings is because it feels good inside. Do not let this poison fool you.

If you have a hard time forgiving others, the love of Christ isn't flowing through you. How do you solve this problem? Start working on your relationship with your heavenly Father so that you can come to know of His great love for you, and then your spirit will respond and His love will begin to flow through you naturally. When that begins to happen, forgiving those who have wronged you will become much easier.

In the village of Bethany, where Jesus shared so much time with Mary, Martha, and their brother, Lazarus, Jesus told Martha that if she believed, she would see the glory of God. Since the start of my transformation, I have seen so much of the glory of God. Wherever we go it has been clear: You can be turned from a mess to a message, from grass to grace.

Without God, I would be nowhere. I would be dead—either a walking corpse or a breathless one. I would never have known what it is to surrender to Him, to weep before Him as a child, to say sorry and to feel His arms hold me, to feel His warm breath that soothes me, to hear Him whisper to me, "It is all right. It is all right. You are forgiven unconditionally. You are loved eternally."

Chapter Eleven

You Will See the Glory of God

It is one thing to try to forgive someone on the occasion when they have hurt you, but it is quite another thing to adopt a *lifestyle* of forgiveness. This takes effort, determination, and sacrifice. To live a lifestyle of forgiveness means choosing to pursue a life of holiness and avoiding the things that could defile you. You have to repent, daily. You have to pray, daily. You have to read the Bible, daily. And you have to forgive others far more frequently than that.

Forgiveness is a process, and it is one that can take years. You might forgive someone once or twice—choosing to not give in to bitterness and to offer grace and kindness—but the wounds we carry within us take far more than Band-Aids and quick kisses to heal. It often takes years to overcome emotional pain, as our own lives—yours as well as mine—make perfectly clear. And when you are dealing with people who deliberately act to harm you, the whole thing just becomes even more complicated and painful.

So why do it? Why forgive?

Forgiveness is like breathing in and breathing out. We must inhale and exhale, asking forgiveness of our own sins and offering it without charge to those who have hurt us. Without it, we suffocate. Without forgiveness we die.

Forgiveness is a serious issue, yet we talk about grudges the way we talk about babies. You can hold a grudge, carry a grudge, bear a grudge, or nurse a grudge. The trouble is, when you nurse something, you feed it, you make it grow, and pretty soon it's a full-grown adult-sized affair that you cannot close the door on when it gets too noisy.

Grudges do not make sense. Why would people pick up something that weighs them down each day and carry it around with them?

"But this person really hurt me!"—that is the usual excuse for holding on to these things. Some of us never seem to realize that it is by holding on to grudges that we enable our debtors to *keep on* hurting us. Even when we know we are supposed to forgive, sometimes it feels too much like giving up something we could not live without.

Abraham Lincoln told a story about a man on his sickbed who had been told by the doctor that he did not have much time to live. He summoned an old friend named Brown with whom he had quarreled bitterly. They had not spoken for years, and from his bed the man talked of how he was going to die soon, of how petty their differences looked in the face of death, and asked if they might be reconciled. The scene moved everyone in the room to tears. Brown clasped the dying man's hands, embraced him, and turned to walk out of the room, a shattered man. Suddenly the man on the sickbed, having one final thought, raised himself up on one elbow and spoke for the last time: "But see here, Brown; if I ever recover, the old grudge still stands."

It is a good story, one that leaves us with a trace of a smile and the words *how foolish!* in our heads. But it is closer to the truth for some of us than we would like to admit. It can be hard to let go of bitterness.

We need to change our view of forgiveness, away from being something that we struggle to give up and toward a lifestyle that sets us free. Forgiveness is not a weapon; it is a revolution—and I hope that by now you are considering joining in the army of revolutionary forgivers, ready to fight bitterness and hatred with love and grace.

When I became a Christian, I found out early on that everywhere I went were people I needed to forgive, and very little has changed in the years since. At first it was the boys who had bullied me when I arrived at school—I had to learn how to live with them. Today I might not be troubled so much by gangs, but there are still many reasons to stop, to pray, and to exhale a little of that same forgiveness that so transformed my own life.

I have found that if there is such a thing as a key to forgiving others, it is found when we grow in God's love. If you reach out to God and seek a deeper relationship with Him, He will draw near to you, and you will find that deeper relationship with Him. God's Word is clear about this fact:

> "And I say unto you, Ask, and it shall be given you;
> seek, and ye shall find; knock, and it shall be opened
> unto you. For every one that asketh receiveth; and
> he that seeketh findeth; and to him that knocketh
> it shall be opened." (Luke 11:9–10)

> Draw nigh to God, and he will draw nigh to you.
> (James 4:8)

The relationship is yours for the taking. Christ wanted this relationship with you so badly that He gave His life for it. Your heavenly Father wants this intimate relationship with you even more than you do. What kind of a relationship does God want with us? He wants an intimate love relationship with us that will empower us to forgive others unconditionally, just as Jesus did with His enemies.

Do not be deceived: Forgiveness is a choice. We must choose to forgive those who have done us wrong and then lay the whole mess in God's hands and leave it there. Give your hurts and hard feelings to Him. Think about Jesus: Even though they murdered Him, some of the last words that left His mouth were, "Father, forgive them" (Luke 23:34). Look at the depth of God's love for us! How can it not begin to change us if we allow ourselves to be truly open to it?

≡

After finishing at school I moved on to Kigezi High School in Kabale. I had no more trouble with gangs and learned far more about God as I joined a revival movement. That movement was formed by the people who had experienced the East African Revival firsthand all those decades before. They were elderly now but very genuine. It was such a change to be surrounded by people who worked to build me up rather than limit my future. Their love was genuine, and when they saw me making mistakes they would tell me how to change.

They taught me how to handle relationships, and all in all it was a very good time of learning from these old men and women.

It was also the first time I came into contact with Bishop Festo Kivengere, a renowned international evangelist who was our local bishop. He became a hero, model, and close friend of mine.

People called him "the Billy Graham of Africa." He had grown up in the southwest region of the country as I had. He was one of the many thousands whose life was transformed during the East African Revival, and he went on to become bishop of Kigezi. He acted as Billy Graham's translator, and according to legend Graham had such faith in Festo that he told him not to worry too much about translating literally and that he trusted him to just get the message across in his own way.

I met Bishop Festo when I was at Kigezi High School, but you may recall that it was not the first time I had seen him. He was there that day in the football stadium when Idi Amin had ranted and raged at the Christians before they were executed. Later Festo wrote about that day:

> February 10 began as a sad day for us in Kabale. People were commanded to come to the stadium and witness the execution.... Death permeated the atmosphere.... A silent crowd of about three thousand was there to watch.... I had permission from the authorities to speak to the men before they died, and two of my fellow ministers were with me.
>
> They brought the men in a truck and unloaded them. They were handcuffed and their feet were

chained. The firing squad stood at attention. As we walked into the center of the stadium, I was wondering what to say…. How do you give the Gospel to doomed men who are probably seething with rage?

We approached them from behind, and as they turned to look at us, what a sight! Their faces were all alight with an unmistakable glow and radiance. Before we could say anything, one of them burst out:

"Bishop, thank you for coming! I wanted to tell you. The day I was arrested, in my prison cell, I asked the Lord Jesus to come into my heart. He came in and forgave me all my sins! Heaven is now open, and there is nothing between me and my God! Please tell my wife and children that I am going to be with Jesus. Ask them to accept him into their lives as I did." The other two men told similar stories, excitedly raising their hands, which rattled their handcuffs.

I felt that what I needed to do was to talk to the soldiers, not to the condemned. So I translated what the men had said into a language the soldiers understood. The military men were standing there with guns cocked and bewilderment on their faces…. [They] were so dumbfounded … that they even forgot to put the hoods over [the men's] faces! The three faced the firing squad standing close together.

They looked toward the people and began to wave,
handcuffs and all. The people waved back. Then
shots were fired, and the three were with Jesus.[1]

Later Bishop Festo had to flee the country to escape Amin's soldiers. Later still he published a book with the title *I Love Idi Amin*.
In it he wrote:

On the cross, Jesus said, "Father, forgive them,
because they don't know what they are doing." As
evil as Idi Amin was, how can I do less toward him?[2]

I had a lot to learn from Bishop Festo, particularly when it
came to talking to people. I knew that forgiveness was important
and that I needed to keep short accounts with people. My problem
was that I was a little too direct. I used to go to people and say, "I
hated you because when you did X and Y, it hurt me. Please forgive
me, as I am sorry…. Oh, and I also forgive you for A and B and C."

Bishop Festo taught me that starting by listing the mistakes and
then asking for forgiveness was not the best approach I could take!
"The truth is good," he told me once, "but it is even better when
presented in an envelope."

He also taught me that forgiveness is like vomiting. When you
are sick you do not choose to vomit rice and leave meat inside you or
vomit salt and hold back the sugar. When you are sick you open your
mouth and vomit out everything indiscriminately. It is the same with
forgiveness; you have to get rid of all that is troubling you inside. You
have to forgive everything.

When our father left we lived like revolutionaries; we did whatever we wanted, we never consulted others, we never thanked anyone. Ours was an independent life, and we felt no need to respect others. I needed to learn how to submit to authority, how to talk to superiors, how to repent without causing offense, and how to sort things out with people in a spirit of love.

During my time at Kigezi High School I also learned how to live by faith, relying on God for food, school fees, and the rest. God provided. He used some missionaries who paid for my fees even though I had no clue they were going to help. Thanks to their support I no longer needed to raise money by working as a porter at school. It restored my self-esteem.

I finished my A-levels in 1986 and went to study at Makerere University in Kampala. I finished three years later with a bachelor of education degree. In my heart I had never really left Kabale or the wider southwestern region of my beautiful homeland. I had chosen to study education, as my heart was for young people and I sensed I would have a ministry of reconciliation with youth.

So during the summers it was all too easy for me to return to Kigezi High School to teach. I would often end up sharing my testimony as well, sharing with people how things had changed for me. It was always a very natural thing for me to do, whether in a crowded classroom or at a larger evangelistic campaign.

I was baptized in the Holy Spirit in 1987, on the ninth of February. I was at a meeting at the university, where Bishop Festo was the chief missioner, and the experience made such a big difference in my life. It left me with a growing sense that I needed to set something up to unite with others. There were many others like me who were passionate about their faith and who also still believed that the Anglican Church had a part to play in the future. We wanted to start up some sort of movement that would reach young people with the gospel and, through them, in time reach their parents.

So, with some friends back at university in Kampala, I began the Kigezi Anglican Youth Missioners. It was like a *back to Jerusalem* ministry, and every holiday we would bring teams back to our home territory to work. Bishop Festo welcomed and supported what we were doing, and because he was a charismatic man who loved young people, I suppose it must have been encouraging to see us working in this way. This ministry later grew into Uganda Anglican Youth Missioners, which has brought a great revival in the Anglican Church of Uganda and extended to the great lakes region of eastern, central, and southern Africa.

One day Bishop Festo challenged me:

"Many younger people leave the Anglican church and head to the Pentecostal churches when they get baptized in the Holy Spirit." He paused. "I am suffering from leukemia, and I do not have long left to live. I would like you to take over in the driving seat of the gospel bus so that the revival does not die with me."

That was our last conversation. The next time I saw him was when I went with others to the airport to receive his coffin when his body was flown back from Nairobi.

From that moment on I decided to walk in Bishop Festo's footsteps. I wanted to connect with younger people, and we ended up witnessing a tremendous revival in Kabale. Sadly that was not all that we saw; the diocese became divided over the revival, and there was a messy split within it. But the Anglican Youth Missioners remained credible, going on to become a national movement. Even today it carries out great work, with an Anglican youth group existing in every university and school, bringing spiritual renewal to the church and reintroducing people to the gifts of the Holy Spirit.

≋

My father died when I was taking my final exams, but even if I had not been busy with study I would not have been any better prepared. His death was unexpected. He was not sick and I had no warning that it was coming. His death caused me great embarrassment, so much so that it is only recently I have started to talk about it.

My father died as a result of a drinking game.

It was a market day, and he was doing what many of my countrymen spend so much of their time doing: He was sitting about, drinking and watching what was going on with his friends. There were four of them there, and somehow the conversation turned to the particular strength of a two-liter bottle of home-brewed alcohol that was on sale in the market. The idle conversation turned to a show of male bravado, and my father bet the others ten thousand Ugandan shillings (about five dollars) that he could drink it all in one go. He did. Then he collected his winnings and went to lie down under a tree. He never woke up.

My father had not given up drinking after he became a Christian. It was very embarrassing for us to lose him like this, and the sorrow and shame lasted for a long time. It was made worse by the fact that I could not get to the funeral due to my final exams at university. But still he died reconciled with his family and relatives, having put right so many of the things that would have caused problems after his death. I would never blame anyone for his death, and I still believe that he went to heaven, even though he died drunk.

I believe that the transformation in his life, the reconciliation with his family and neighbors, was genuine. I know some believe an alcohol-related death will take someone to hell, but I am not so sure I agree with that. The Bible is not so black and white. While it condemns drunkenness, it condones drinking wine in moderation. There are some people who do not drink in public but who drink a little at home, including Christians in Uganda. Alcohol remains a very dangerous thing, of course; it can make you addicted; it can make you sexually immoral or violent. Last year in Uganda eighty men killed their wives while drunk, and thirty-seven wives killed their husbands in self-defense. Uganda now has the second-highest rate of road traffic accidents in the world because of reckless driving caused by the influence of alcohol. The impact can be devastating, which is why the old revival movement declared drinking alcohol a sin in 1936. From then on no born-again Christian was supposed to drink, and the change has proved very positive with people.

My father's death left a big impact on us children. It was devastating, but it was not an isolated incident. My aunt Lillian died through the abuse of alcohol; my two brothers, James and Robert, as well; one of my uncles; and my grandfather and great-grandfather. I feel sad when I admit that most of the people in my family are alcoholics. It is a family stronghold that many of us have given in to. That and polygamy. Thankfully I can say that I have been delivered from both of them by Jesus.

I used to love drinking, even though it would make me sick and incontinent. But becoming a Christian changed things for me, teaching me that my body is a temple of the Holy Spirit. And so I decided to stop. I did not want to take a step closer to the state in which my father committed most of his crimes. When I lived in the UK, where Christians drink without a problem, it was tempting for me to go back, but I had escaped this bondage and did not want to get caught up again. I wanted to be an example to my children. None of them drink now, for which I am very grateful.

Because I worked at Kigezi High School during every summer vacation while at university, it was not surprising that I started out as a teacher there after I graduated. At the same time as teaching I was also speaking and preaching at churches throughout the district on the weekends. Within a few months this was all I was doing—teaching during the week and preaching on the weekend. It was too much, not least because I had met a woman I loved deeply and was intending to marry. How could I be a good husband if I was never around? I quit teaching in the high school and moved to help educate trainee teachers instead. I taught at National Teachers College of Kabale and later at Kakoba in Mbarara. That gave me more time for preaching … and for Connie.

I met Connie during my gap year in 1986. There was a war between Museveni's rebels and the government of the day, which resulted in the rebels taking power and the whole of the west of Uganda being cut off. I went to teach in a girls' high school in Rukungiri—the same town in which I had studied and become a Christian. At the school in which I was teaching I met her, the beautiful head girl of the school. She was born again and looked after the Scripture Union ministry in the school. The head teacher allowed me to take students out twice each month for evangelistic weekends. I was leading a team, and Connie often came along at my invitation. Of course I did not know I wanted to marry her then, but we connected well.

Connie was born in an abusive home. Her father was an alcoholic. Although he was not a polygamist, he was a very violent womanizer, and Connie, her mother, and her siblings spent a lot of their time sleeping in the bush to avoid being beaten. Her father was such a prolific and reckless drinker that he sold his wife's bed to get money to drink. He even sold the iron sheets from the roof just so that he could pay for his drink. Everyone in the village saw that the family was in a terrible state, and when I met her, Connie had to work at school for her fees. I helped out with the fees while on my gap year, though little did I know that I was investing in a future marriage. I also had no idea that later on this would be another family I would see transformed by Christ. Eventually Connie's father became a Christian, and today he is both an evangelist and one of my closest friends.

After she left school Connie and I grew close. In time I decided to propose, and since her father worked in the post office, I gave him a letter to pass on to his daughter. He was curious and asked her what it was all about. Connie knew that I was a traditional man and that a letter from me could mean only one thing. She explained, and he was happy about it. He thought I was a good boy.

His wife felt otherwise. I believe her words on hearing of the proposal were something like "over my dead body." She thought I was common and way too inferior for her daughter.

In Uganda sons-in-law are supposed to gain great respect from mothers-in-law. A son-in-law is supposed to be a counselor, a confidant, a supporting male—there to step in should the father-in-law pass on. Connie's mother wanted none of this from me.

Things were no better by the time Connie and I were married. The wedding day itself was horrific. I went to pick up my future wife, but there was her mother, standing sentry at the entrance to the house. She was a dam across the door, refusing to allow either me in or her daughter out. And from her mouth flowed vile verbal abuse. She cursed and swore at me, and it was only when Connie pushed her hard at her back that she stumbled and allowed my fiancée to escape and make it to the car. As we sped off—leaving the flower girl and the matron behind—her words had already inflicted deep wounds on us both. All the way from Connie's home in Rukungiri to our wedding in Kabale we sat in silence broken only by the sounds of our crying.

That was quite a test. How do you forgive someone who does something so deliberate to hurt you? Connie had warned me that her mother was not happy, but I never thought she would be quite so rude to us. I never imagined she would behave in such a way.

Later—years later—we did reconcile, and we asked each other's forgiveness. Now I am close to her, and she says I am one of the best in-laws she has ever had. But at the time the pain I experienced was immense. Despite the fact that my father and I had long been reconciled, this repeat of a parent figure pouring out abuse cut me to the core.

I had been dropped by a previous fiancée as well, which had devastated me. We were friends for three years, and out of the blue she terminated the relationship. I was so wounded because it was like adding an insult to an injury of rejection. After prayer and fasting, the Lord told me that the best wine comes last. Indeed Connie came as the best wine. Yet my marriage to Connie did not have the easiest of starts; in addition to all of this, we had to work through my fears and insecurities around sex that were the consequence of my being abused by my sister. But we persevered. We prayed. We wept, we talked—with each other as well as wise friends, relatives, and leaders—and we trusted that God would heal. And He did, fully and without reservation. I call Connie "Miss Uganda 1991," for she captivated my heart with her beauty. That this beautiful, faithful girl would marry such a wrecked boy could only be because of the redeeming blood of Jesus.

After we were married I worked for Scripture Union as a traveling secretary for the west of Uganda. There were about two thousand primary and secondary schools in my region, and from 1992 to 1994 I visited as many of them as I could. I would travel and give my testimony, nothing more than that. I cannot tell you how many came to the Lord, but there were many, many people who did. I used to keep records, and from 1989 to 1997 I noted that I had led fifty thousand people to Christ. After that I stopped counting.

Working with Scripture Union was easily the happiest time in my life at that point. I had a sense of fulfillment, and I was speaking to students who were going through difficulties that I cared about—domestic violence, bitterness, anger, and hatred. I spoke with so many victims of rape, so many who had been defiled or molested by uncles and aunts and sisters and brothers. I still give thanks today for that time, for so many people with whom I was able to talk and pray. I thank God for the privilege of seeing Him take that which I thought was decayed and using it to bring others closer to wholeness—and closer to Him.

Chapter Twelve

Lazarus, Come Out!

"I beg your pardon?"

I was standing in the office of the general secretary of the Bible Society in Uganda. I had just come from a training course in Bible distribution and marketing at the University of Zambia. Outside was the usual noise, dust, and chaos of Kampala, a city made up of lives thrown together like a pack of playing cards released into a storm. Inside the office the occupant had done his best to keep the city's disorder out. A lace curtain softened the window, and the dark wood desk was weighed down by neat piles of papers and small towers of Bibles. The walls were covered in homemade, handwritten posters that outlined the leadership structure within the organization. My boss's name was always written a little larger and with a little more care than the others. He repeated his statement to me.

"Your performance is below average, your work is poor, and we cannot continue to employ you. Go and try your luck elsewhere."

The room was small, and the man who was telling me that he was no longer my employer appeared smaller still. He remained calm, delivering his verdict without emotion or any obvious signs of malice. Yet nothing could suppress my anger. Nothing could keep the city's chaos from this room.

During my work for various Christian organizations I have come to learn that forgiveness cannot be a one-time decision. I have discovered this as a father as well, and of course as a sibling and a son. But the lessons learned in offices like those of the head of the Bible Society have been some of the hardest to take. The Bible says that bad times will never fail to come; I suppose I never imagined they would come so frequently from those working for the wider church.

Back in 1994 I was in the office of the Bible Society's general secretary because I was working as the Society's national distribution officer. I had started well, and they had sent me to Tanzania to attend a course in marketing and Bible distribution. I went, studied hard, and performed well. They said I was the best-performing student.

I reported back to Kampala, standing before the neat desk and lace-fringed window, expecting to have my six-month probationary period signed off as a success. I had sold all the Bibles I had been given and believed I had performed well, fulfilling my potential throughout the preceding months. I was sure I was working well, and yet my boss was telling me otherwise. My boss was giving me the sack.

I was stunned. I had no inclination that this was going to happen, and with a wife and now two children to look after, the loss of my job—and the home that came with it—was a colossal blow. I had never been that angry since becoming a Christian, nor have I experienced such rage in the years that have passed since that time.

I was mad at them for ignoring the truth that I was doing well, mad at them for duping me this way. Once more I was pulled down from the truck and left shocked and saddened at the roadside.

I considered appealing to the board. I felt that I had a case, that my dismissal was unfair, but what sort of victory would the board be able to grant me? I would still have to stand in this office, still have to submit to this man, and more than likely still end up at some point in the future being told again to "try my luck" elsewhere.

Later I discovered that at the time he sacked me, my boss was fearful for his job and was on a warning for his own performance. Later still we were reconciled, but we will get to that in good time. As I left the office of the Bible Society that afternoon, I wondered how to tell Connie that we were to be evicted from our house—our beautiful, well-appointed house that even had electricity. How to tell her that we would be on the move so soon after we had started this new life together in Kampala.

A friend reminded me that it is God who commands our destinies, not board members or paranoid bosses. I was not a lost cause, and there was no need for an appeal, no need to fight. And so I did what I had done so many times before when times of crisis loomed: I went back to my beautiful homeland around Kabale. I became a teacher at Kigezi High School once more. The only problem was finding somewhere to live. We could only afford an old abandoned house that had been home to nothing more than cows and an informal public toilet for almost a year. It was empty when we arrived, but the odor was repulsive and overpowering. We were now moving from our luxury bungalow to a toilet! Even the driver who had transported us and our possessions from Kampala wept with us.

We fetched water to clean the house, wondering through the tears what God had in store for us. But my son, even though he was small, sang one simple song over and over again: "If not for Jesus, I would not be here."

Over time the place became our home. Despite the fact that the roof was missing in many rooms, the house became a refuge for us.

A few months later, a friend from England sent me a check with a letter that said, "They shall stay in houses they did not build." For some reason (I must not have read the letter properly), I wondered whether God was about to provide somewhere else for us to live. So I banked the check, and Connie and I started to look for a plot where we could build a house of our own.

On the way from the bank, cash in hand, I met the owner of the house we had been staying in since we arrived. He was a great friend of mine and a mentor. I knew that his wife was due to fly to America to start her PhD, and I accompanied him now to say good-bye to her.

As we were walking he told me she had just found out that she was unable to fly out, as she had not raised enough money. "She is not going," he said. "We are five million short."

"Oh," I said. "That is not good."

"Do you want to buy the house from us?"

I did, but there was no way this would be possible. Apart from the fact that it was in need of much work, it was far too expensive for us. I shrugged as I replied, "Eh! That is too much money for me. It must be worth twenty million." Suddenly I stopped as I remembered what I was carrying in my pocket. "But I do have some cash here. We are going to buy a plot somewhere and start to build."

"How much do you have?"

"I have five million."

His eyes popped wide and his jaw dropped. "Eh!" he shouted. "Stay there!"

He disappeared inside to rouse his wife. She was lying on their bed, depressed. She had been due to leave for the airport that afternoon, and the disappointment at not going was too much for her.

I could hear her husband from where I was sitting outside. "Do you know that God has brought an angel here? The amount you need is exactly what Birungi has. We have abandoned that house anyway ... why do we not give it to him as a gift?"

His wife rushed outside and grabbed me, shouting, "Where is the money?" I handed it over. Quickly we completed the paperwork, and I returned home—to our home.

"Where is the money?" said Connie as I entered. "If you hang on to it for too long, people will come and ask you to loan them stuff, and it will soon disappear."

"I have a letter for you, Connie." I gave her the contract and stepped outside to look at the home we did not build but which now was ours.

Eventually Connie came out to join me. There were tears all down her face as she spoke to me.

"Do you remember what our son sang as we were crying when we arrived here? 'If not for Jesus I would not be here.' That is precisely what God meant by all this: to remind us that it all comes from Him."

God's restoration went even further than that. After I lived through four months of bitterness and anger, the general secretary of the Bible Society was sacked. He was so shocked that his heart started to give him pain and he was rushed to the hospital. I was in Kampala at the time and a mutual acquaintance told me the news. He also challenged me: What would I say at this man's grave if I did not put things right with him?

I was reluctant, but it was good advice. When I arrived, he wept as he apologized for sacking me and explained that he was motivated by a fear that I would one day succeed him. He admitted that he had persuaded the board to fire me, confessed that he was wrong, and asked for my forgiveness.

God gave me the courage to forgive, and we were reconciled. God healed him too, and he ended up as headmaster of a secondary school when I was working in the education department of the diocese of Kigezi. Today he leads revival meetings, and he often talks to people about our time together and the power of forgiveness. Forgiveness is not about merely being tolerant, pretending that nothing happened, or being diplomatic in public. Forgiveness is a deliberate act of the will, a full pardon, an act of love that is the key to freedom.

≡

You can repent of all your sins until you are hoarse. You can confess your faith to all, pray without ceasing, give everything you have for the work of God, read the Bible every day, and still block God's forgiveness by an unforgiving heart. No amount of repenting, confessing, praying, or reading the Word will ever cover over, atone for, or excuse unforgiveness. There is nothing you can do that can take the place of forgiveness.

The waterfall at Kisiizi had failed to claim my life; instead the hospital that lies at its foot was the place where so much healing among my family, including my aunt and my father, took place. It was also the place where I met some wonderful *muzungu* from England who were working in the hospital. They were kind to me and helped me get the contacts and the money to travel to the United Kingdom to study.

≋

When I arrived in Britain it was a terrible culture shock. I thought that people would greet me when I went into their church, but on my first Sunday in the country I entered the local church like a ghost. Not one person spoke to me. It was a terrible shock, and it did not happen just once. I attended the church for a whole month, and still I passed in and out of the doors with not one person acknowledging me.

I was enrolled in a two-year course at a Bible college, and on good advice I tried another church—St. Andrew's Chorleywood. As I passed through the doors I was asked my name and where I was from. I told them.

"You're from Uganda? Do you know Bishop Lyth?"

I did not, but I had heard of him. He was the founder and first bishop of the diocese of Kigezi, the man who had laid the foundations on which the East African Revival was able to thrive.

The greeter at the door knew Bishop Lyth. "He has been a pastor here ever since he retired. Would you like to meet him?"

Within a few days I was sitting in a comfortable English drawing room, drinking tea and talking Rukiga—the language of my people—with a man whose legacy had strengthened my own history as well as the history of thousands of others.

But Bishop Lyth was not the only connection with Kabale that this London suburb had to offer. I was told that there was another church nearby that was well loved by Bishop Festo. He would preach at Emmanuel Church Northwood, and his personal secretary was still a member of the congregation there. As I arrived they were very welcoming, the vicar asking me to come up to the front and say hello. As I approached I spotted a picture of Bishop Festo on the wall, and I was happy to oblige when they asked if I would give a little of my testimony. They said I had five minutes, but I was on African time: I took fifteen. But people wept as they heard what I had to say.

I was invited to return and give my story in full the following Thursday night. The impact it had was immense; people asked me to go to their houses to speak to their children, their husbands, or their wives. The vicar asked me to come and speak to people who were suffering from depression, and I am still in contact with some of those I was privileged to pray with and see Jesus heal.

I started to walk the streets, praying for the people living in their large houses whose doors were always shut. Often I felt God push me to knock on one of those doors. Most of the time what happened would be fairly brief. Once their eyes settled on me their faces would be set with fear, so I would quickly introduce myself as "Medad from Uganda." I would ask if I could pray for them. They often said no. I later found out that there had been some Nigerian con men at work in the area, and that had made residents wary of any strange African men acting unusually. It did not bother me, though; I was just going bananas for Jesus.

One time my introductory speech was cut short as the lady on the other side slammed the door hard in my face. She must have felt convicted, as she opened it again a few moments later.

"Why are you here? I have heard so many people talk about you. What is it about?"

I told her my testimony—the short version! I told her about grace, forgiveness, and the ability to start again.

She started to weep. She had separated from her husband many years earlier, and he was now in the hospital, dying. She asked me, "Do you think my husband would forgive me?"

"Why not?" I said. "The moment you accept Christ and ask forgiveness, ask Him for His hand of peace; your husband will forgive you."

Some days later her son drove her the four hours up to Manchester to visit her estranged husband in the hospital. That very night she called me and told me how she had cried in his arms for an hour. And she told me that before she could ask for his forgiveness, he apologized to her for mistreating her and asked her to forgive him.

I was able to attend his funeral a few weeks later. He had died at peace with his wife, who spoke words of powerful grace and healing in front of the mourners.

≋

During my two years living in the West I never overcame the sense of shock at the way people dressed, especially on the odd occasion that I visited a beach. They were—by African standards—naked and did not appear to be ashamed at all. I talked to my friends and they said it was normal, but I was still shocked. The divorce rate was equally worrying, as was the number of children who wandered around the streets, doing nothing in the day and embracing trouble at night. I would talk to them, too, and I developed a pub ministry as a result, talking to young people and bringing them to the church.

I made the mistake of thinking that a Bible college was a place where students would dedicate themselves to the pursuit of a more godly way of living, where they would sacrifice the appeal of the world in favor of getting closer to God. But the way they behaved was just like those who attended a secular university. I saw people drinking and behaving in inappropriate ways with their boyfriends and girlfriends. But I made many friends. I knew from my own experience that God calls His people to deal in grace far more than judgment. As the principal told me, God does not call the qualified, but He qualifies the called.

≣

Living in England with my wife and children was good in many ways, but, despite being offered a job as a youth pastor, I felt strongly that I had a role to play here in my own country. And I wanted my children to grow up in Africa. Children in the West are given too much freedom, in my opinion, and there is little sense of right and wrong. They have too much freedom with too little framework for their behavior. Connie and I talked about it for four months, and we decided to come back to Uganda. And so I began work for the diocese.

This was made possible because in England I had met the new bishop of Kigezi, Bishop George. He and I had got on well, or at least that is what I thought at the time. He had offered to ordain me when I returned to Uganda, and having felt as though I had been through a period of revival within my soul while abroad, I was excited to see what was in store for me once I was back home in Uganda. Surely there were even more exciting things ahead.

In 1998 my family and I returned once more to Kabale, ahead of my proposed ordination. I was funded by clergy back in England and took on what I thought would be the interim role of diocesan education secretary. Within a few months I would become the Reverend Medad Birungi and could set about taking on some fresh challenges. While I was settling into my new job, I presented my thesis on charismatic renewal to the bishop and his staff; soon afterward things started to go wrong. They did not like what they read and called me a heretic. I kept preaching the gospel, healing the sick, and casting out demons, but my hopes for ordination were dashed. The bishop refused to ordain me.

The same thing happened the next year. And the next. For three years I was told that I would be ordained along with the next batch, but each time the plans were put on hold. I felt rejected, abandoned, and useless, now that the church had also rejected me. Bitterness and unforgiveness were rekindled, and it made me depressed again and again. But I kept repenting and forgiving. My relationship with the bishop deteriorated, particularly as the teacher and orphan sponsorship programs that my department was running were attracting increasing overseas support. There was also greater jealousy and envy from the clergy. I became increasingly stressed, until I got a scholarship for a PhD and asked the bishop to release me. I left the diocese but kept lecturing at Uganda Christian University, Kabale Campus, part-time to pay for my wife's education, as she was working toward a degree there. Until I was fired. They told me that since I had left the diocese, I should not teach in a church-founded institution.

For a long time I had wanted to start an evangelistic association, to work alongside the increasing number of people from the West who wanted to visit Uganda to help preach and teach. Eventually Swallow Evangelistic Revival Ministries was born. It was a non-denominational organization, though we did ask the bishop to be our patron. He agreed on the condition that the diocese would oversee it. We knew we could not limit it that way, and more trouble followed as the relationship between us suffered further.

I started to exercise spiritual gifts, particularly healings and deliverance, but the more these areas of my life seemed to grow, the greater the tensions between the bishop and me became. When I resigned my post as diocesan education secretary, my wife's job with Kigezi High School was also terminated. In 2002 the bishop called a synod to ask people whether they thought I was forming a heretical cultic movement, and he advised the synod not to have anything to do with me or Swallow Ministries. The majority said yes, I was a heretic. They thought I was going to follow in the footsteps of a Ugandan Catholic cult called the Restoration of the Ten Commandments. In 2000 they had burned 1,500 people alive in a church. The diocese claimed I was just as dangerous as the priest who had started the cult and suggested that they should not associate with our ministry or me. They stopped me from preaching;

almost overnight I found myself in exile in Kampala. For the sake of peace the organization was disbanded. But the root of bitterness started to grow again.

Life was difficult once more. My wife and children had to leave our beautiful home in Kabale because some of the local Christians had taken to intimidating them, whispering accusations, and blackening their names. All the rejections from the past lined up and added their force to this latest blow from my spiritual father figure, the bishop, together with the clergy and Christians who followed his lead. I suffered from the poison of malicious, unjustified accusations, and the rejection did not stop when we left the diocese. I had a scholarship for further study, but it was canceled. I went to work at Kampala International University but was sacked after one term. I was invited to attend an interview at Kyambogo University, but they canceled the appointment without explanation. I managed to get another job, one that came with accommodation that had been provided by a kind *muzungu* who knew me, but the employer ended up taking the accommodation away from us when the contract was terminated.

We were financially crippled and had to live on charity. We had four children and no job. We were living in people's houses, sleeping on the floors of whatever friends we could find. It was difficult and served only to increase the sense of bitterness and anger within me. Eventually we were saved by a kind church that paid for our accommodation and by some faithful overseas believers who supported us for two years.

But what happened next was what really destroyed and shattered me.

The archbishop of Uganda at the time—a man called His Grace Livingstone Nkoyoyo—was supportive of me. And I liked him. He took me on and sent me on a short course at Uganda Christian University so that he could ordain me. At last my dream of being ordained was about to be realized. I approached September 2003 with my confidence high; if the head of the entire Anglican Church in Uganda was behind me, what could possibly go wrong? I invited people from all over to attend the ceremony. There were guests from back in Kabale, Rwanda, Burundi, Kenya, and even the United Kingdom—two hundred in all.

On the night before our Sunday service ordination, I gathered along with the other ordinands to make our vows. Suddenly the archbishop was called out. I was suspicious, even more so when a friend from Kabale in the room warned me that something was happening.

I was called into a meeting with Connie. All the big men from the church in Uganda were there. They told me that the bishop had objected to my ordination. He had repeated his accusations of heresy and had threatened to resign if they went ahead and ordained me. Their verdict was as sharp as that knife my uncle had used to slash my foot as I grazed on bananas at the top of the tree: "We are canceling your ordination until you sort things out with Bishop George."

Connie screamed and fell to the ground. She was having trouble breathing, and my own sense of being crushed was momentarily lifted as together with a friend I struggled to carry her out to a car.

But the feelings could not be buried forever. The sense of devastation was immense, as potent as any poison I had ever feared. All the old bitterness returned: from my father, from my uncles, from my aunts, from my mother-in-law, from the Bible Society. All the anger, humiliation, and shame returned. What would I tell people? How could I explain this to them? I wept all night. Connie recovered after thirty minutes as we were driven home, where two hundred visitors were waiting for us in a preordination night vigil. We were all exhausted, overcome by stress, humiliation, fear, anger, bitterness, and depression. Connie was so weak that four men had to carry her to her bed. When the cheering crowd of visitors, friends, and relatives were told what had happened, they wailed and cried; others screamed, and my sister fainted. Hearing the cries of all those people sank me into bitterness again.

I cried all night. It was only in the morning that I was saved by a phone call from Bishop Henry Orombi, the archbishop-elect. He told me to meet him right away, and when we met I cried in his loving arms. After twenty minutes I stopped. He encouraged me, prayed for me, and asked me to attend the ordination service anyway.

I turned up at the next day's ceremony. The archbishop stood up and explained the situation to the assembled congregation, who knew nothing of the previous evening's events. "We were going to ordain Medad Birungi, but there are problems with his bishop that need to get sorted out. Pray for him. Pray for them both. But we are going to commission him as a lay evangelist."

Months passed, and eventually I received a job offer from the vice chancellor of Kyambogo University, the place that had canceled my appointment. The fuss at the ordination ceremony had set him straight, and he offered me a job.

Perhaps it might seem an odd thing to spend so much time and energy pursuing ordination, but for me it offered the potential to work much more effectively within the country I so dearly love. Perhaps it is a system that will not last for much longer, but for now the Anglican Church in Uganda—as well as in much of Africa—is a powerful force with the potential to serve and support millions. To work outside of its power structures would have been to turn my back on my spiritual forefathers and my spiritual heritage.

Mercifully it took only another year for me to finally be ordained. In 2004 His Grace Henry Orombi, now the archbishop of the province of the Church of Uganda and bishop of the diocese of Kampala, a long-standing friend and mentor, made it possible. I had worked with him in evangelistic missions and conventions and in the healing and deliverance ministry, and I used to translate for him whenever he came to preach in western Uganda. On my ordination he declared to me and to Connie, "The time of tears and humiliation is over. The time of joy and glory has come!"

He was right. He has been a loving, caring, affirming, close, and dependable father to me. We love him, and we are proud of him. He has done an incredible work in restoring my confidence and vision of reviving the Anglican Church of Uganda. He is not only my bishop but a very close friend and spiritual father. He has prayed for me, trusted me, and protected me. He made me an acting chaplain of a big chapel even when I was still a deacon. My ministry flourished, and the church grew in quality and quantity and became one of the fastest-growing churches in Uganda. After five years of a joyful, fulfilling, and anointed ministry, he promoted me to my current post of diocesan missions, evangelism, and church-planting coordinator for the diocese of Kampala. I like this job, and I am now coordinating twenty-three congregations in the areas of mission and evangelism, discipleship and church planting, healing and deliverance. Many people are getting healed, delivered, and reconciled.

When I look back upon this journey now I can so clearly see God at work. He was never absent. He never went missing. He has always been with me. How else could anyone explain the growth of the church I planted? We tried to practice what had once been branded heretical by the bishop, bringing together the best of the Anglican tradition with openness to the Holy Spirit. I found a chapel growing with a congregation of some one thousand members, and by the time I left, there were about six thousand of us. We started with a small church and built a huge cathedral. God and God alone was the architect.

≋

My journey along the winding roads of forgiveness was not over. In many ways I know it never will be—I still have to practice forgiveness today. But as the church grew, I knew I had to put things right with Bishop George.

So I telephoned him and told him I had forgiven him. He said, "Okay," but nothing more. Six months later he met with Connie and me at Namirembe Guest House in Kampala. We met and sat and sorted our things out. Almost. The reconciliation did not really take place—he did not tell people in Kabale that we had fixed things, and the ban on my ministering in the area remained in place.

And then in 2005 there came the final breakthrough. I smile today when I remember the setting: an East African Revival convention meeting in Kabale. I was asked to be the translator for a visiting *muzungu* speaker who insisted I attend. He spoke about the episode from the Gospels when Jesus and His disciples were caught up in a great storm. They needed a great prayer to be answered by a great person in order to have a great landing.

Holiness, integrity, truth. These had been the hallmarks of those involved in the great revival of the past, but they were not the only traits that were valued. Repentance and forgiveness had featured just as highly. There must have been something in the air during that meeting, but I was not so aware. All I knew was that this was the first time I had taken to a stage in Kabale in years, and the conflicts had hurt me. Forgiveness had cost me.

The speaker finished his sermon, and the bishop walked onto the stage. As he reached the front he asked me to stay where I was and not to sit down just yet. And then it came—out of nowhere, it seemed to me. The bishop, in front of thousands, said the words I longed for but never thought I would hear. He said he was sorry for all he had wrongly done against me. He asked for my forgiveness. He asked for reconciliation. Then he announced that I was free to preach in any church in the diocese.

How can I explain the joy and peace between us that followed? I accepted and asked him to forgive me as well, which he did. I also asked for forgiveness from those who had been wounded by our conflicts, and the bishop asked other bishops from western Uganda to come up onto the stage and welcome me. I forgave him publicly, and Connie was called up to the front: It was like a pair of prodigals coming home! People embraced one another and sang, and there were tears after tears flowing from every one of us.

The bishop and I embraced for a long time. The tombstone had been rolled away, and Lazarus had come out. Just as Jesus told the mourners to unbind His friend and let him go, so too has the bishop continued to release me. Since that meeting he has continually invited me to preach in meetings, retreats, and conventions in his diocese. The bishop is now a very close friend of mine, and I love him, trust him, and am proud of him. He is special to me.

I had to repent of my bitterness and anger toward the bishop, and doing so added to the long list of things from which the Lord has released me: family hurts, economic hurts, academic hurts, work-related hurts, political hurts, religious hurts, sexually related hurts, and sectarian-related hurts. I am now healed, delivered, and free, and I have realized that the only way for us to be released from the past is to forgive.

What does it mean to forgive? It means obeying a direct command from God. It means following Jesus' example. It means being open to the healing and deliverance that follow. It means embracing repentance, reconciliation, and brokenness. It means seeing a release of prayer and intercession, an increase in joyfulness, and a radical rise in missionary zeal. To forgive is to grow, to live, to love. To forgive is to follow Jesus. To forgive is to leave behind the tomb and to walk out, surrounded by fresh air and new life, toward the open arms of a waiting, loving God.

Back on that stage, with all the holy chaos breaking out around us, my face covered in tears, I knew I was in the middle of a life-changing experience. The bishop's words were simple, as was our embrace, but it was nothing short of a revolution.

Chapter Thirteen

Take Off the Grave Clothes

I suppose you could say I had something in common with Lazarus. We both thought life was over. We both thought the ground had finally claimed us. We both were wrong.

Lazarus's story starts in Bethany, just two miles from Jerusalem. There he lived with his sisters, Mary and Martha, and played out his life. We know their story well: We know how they loved Jesus; we know how He loved them. We know this loving community was so strong that whenever Jesus visited Jerusalem He stayed in their home, resting in their company, finding restoration, anointing, and peace. Nothing has really changed in the two thousand years that have passed. God still wants loving homes and open communities like the one His Son was attracted to in Bethany. God is still after united families who can draw others to them. Unity still attracts a blessing, just as it did back then.

Despite all that history, I imagine it still must have been difficult for them to hold on to their trust in Jesus when things started to go wrong. But they did the right thing; they knew Jesus would help their dying brother.

This is where my story—and maybe yours—stops being similar to Lazarus's. When things go wrong, whom do we reach for first? Where is our hope located? Is prayer our first response to the crisis, or do we turn to the medics or the police or the self-help guru? You might flinch at such a charge. You might say, "But I pray about everything, and any crisis will see me on my knees." A lot of us have learned to pray as a response to troubles. The only problem is that often the prayers last only as long as we are on our knees. As soon as we find our feet we take matters into our own hands. Once things get better our desire to pray evaporates. We are probably unaware that we are doing it, but we attempt to make ourselves feel better by shopping or eating or drinking. We may start with prayer, but our self-reliance soon takes over.

But not Mary and Martha. When the very fabric of their family was threatened, they called for Jesus. And then they waited.

Could we learn to do the same?

I was not patient. I did not trust God. I did not believe in the power of Jesus to transform. Instead I simply wanted to die. As time passed, those feelings grew stronger, but they were accompanied by new responses to pain and troubles. We turned to witch doctors when we began to worry. We went to so many of them—all the time trying to stir up so much evil instead of searching for the goodness of God—that my chest is covered with scars as a result. Ours was not the way of Mary and Martha. Ours was a party of bitterness, hatred, and control.

We know the story of Lazarus did not progress in quite the way Mary and Martha were hoping. Jesus was away—there was nothing unusual about that—but then Lazarus got sick, and Jesus was absent.

What was worse was that when they sent Him a message and urged Him to return, Jesus did not show up. The Bible tells us that He did a strange thing. He did nothing. For two days He waited. We do not know what He did in the time, but we do know this: At the end of the waiting, He knew Lazarus was dead and buried. They asked Jesus to come, and He waited until their brother was dead.

We might not like it, but the truth that applies to every one of us is this: Just as Jesus was aware of Lazarus's life and death, so He is also aware of us: our sin, our weaknesses, our complaints, our pornography, our pain, our disappointment.

And just as we might not be comfortable with the idea of Jesus being aware of every aspect of our lives, we also do not like it when it appears as if the Lord withdraws from us. We do not like to be left surrounded by the corpses of the latest trials and struggles. We do not like to be reminded of the gap between what we hoped for from God and what He actually delivered. Days can turn into weeks, even months, and still it seems that our Father has chosen to delay His return to us, to hold off His presence, to keep back His voice and hands and help. Our sicknesses get worse, our pressures mount even higher, and still Jesus delays coming to our side.

So often at times like this it appears that the only option open to us is to feed on bitterness. That is what I did—for twenty years. And it left me alone. We often find ourselves alone after we have been disappointed by others, let down by those we thought were going to do better this time. But people will let us down—churches, too, which are nothing more than a collection of people—and our relationships with them will suffer. Our gurus may fall and our heroes may fail. Yet if turning to God is a familiar response, something built into the muscles and nerves of our faith, then even those darkest, loneliest nights will be relieved of the chill of isolation. We will find God in the darkness because we have known Him so well in the light.

You know by now that I did none of this when I was younger. I bore a grudge and harbored hatred. I became so good at this that when someone suggested I needed to forgive, the anger that rose within me was nothing short of volcanic.

It cannot have been easy for Mary and Martha to hold on to the hope that Jesus would heal their brother. And the death of Lazarus must have been a moment they had feared with increasing terror and confusion. They had sent for Jesus—why had He not come?

For Mary and Martha, as well as for us, the greatest truth at that time was this: God's delay is not a denial. God may delay in doing things, but that time lag does not mean He has abandoned or denied us. No matter how long we have been praying, no matter how long we have been waiting, God will show. In time—His time, perfect and boundless—God will be with us. No matter how heavy the sorrow or how long the winter, God will return.

We may have experienced the sense that things have wandered too far off course. We may be plagued with self-doubt and wonder if we really were right to count ourselves as close to Jesus. Had we not told others of His love for us? Weren't we the ones who were happy to welcome Him into every aspect of our lives? And now what? What is this silence, this absence that has fallen across our lives? Where is He? Why has He abandoned us? Why is there so much death and decay at our feet? Why are we still wearing these grave clothes?

But a funeral may not be all that it seems—especially when the body goes missing. We may think our hopes have died; we may think our dreams are just waiting to be buried. But God has other plans. For Him, our self-declared funeral can become a resurrection.

Our hope is never truly dead. It is merely asleep.

I had no idea of this as the bruises started to cause me pain when my mother and sisters and I remained in the dirt and dust at the side of the road. I had no idea that this point would be forever marked in my mind as the start of an incredible journey. I had no idea that this was not a funeral but the first glimmer of light on what would become the day of my rebirth.

Lazarus discovered this. He learned that, when we see a funeral, God sees a maternity ward. When we see decay, He sees forgiveness. When we see a boy cowering at the side of the road and hoping to die, He sees a life ahead that is full of beauty and hope and grace.

And so this is a book about two words: forgiveness and revolution. Do those words fit? Are they not just a little too distant, too far apart, to really work together?

History tells us that this cannot work, that the famous revolutions of the past have very little to do with forgiveness. Was forgiveness overflowing in the hearts of those who cheered as guillotines sliced their way through the French aristocracy? Were those early American soldiers stuffing their muskets with pity and mercy as they drove back the English soldiers? Were the Russian tsars shot because of forgiveness? I do not think so.

But just because the best-known revolutions of the past have been fueled by anger and hatred does not mean that forgiveness is not a revolutionary tool. In fact, I want to suggest that of all the weapons and the tactics, of all the guns and the bombs, the most revolutionary thing of all is forgiveness.

Of all the people in the world, there are none stronger than the people who are able to forgive.

Of all the change in the world, there is none more lasting than the change that comes from hearts full of grace and love, hearts that choose forgiveness instead of blaming and bitterness.

And of all the revolutionary acts that have ever taken place, it was the voluntary death—and resurrection—of Jesus that transformed life and death so completely.

≋

It is almost time for this book to finish. I have told you nearly all my story, although, like any African preacher, I could go on for much longer. But I would like to end by telling you about the latest work to which I believe God's hand has directed me. My mother died in 2002, but she died a happy woman and had a glorious funeral. The bishop led the service. It was like a convention. She died after seeing all her daughters marry and four of my children born. I miss her greatly.

This new work started when I was traveling around various communities in southwestern Uganda. I saw so many children who were going through almost the same experience I knew as a child: domestic violence, extreme poverty, rejection, polygamy, abuse. I felt a burden upon me and knew I could do something to give hope to these children at risk.

Their poverty was—and is—so like mine. Across our country are children who have no access to school, who are on the streets, who go hungry, whose distended bellies are signs of malnutrition rather than full stomachs. They suffer from jiggers, head lice, and adults who see them as easy labor to be beaten and physically harassed at will.

I needed to begin a project where even just a few of them could be safe and have an education. Just as Connie and I both felt that Christianity had transformed us, so we knew we should build our work on solid Christian principles. We knew we should take in children and hand them over at eighteen, having instilled in them Christian values and restored their self-esteem; having renewed their thinking and broken cultural bondages, lifting them to a level where they can reach their potential because they know their position in Christ. He becomes the source of their security, self-worth, and significance.

So we established World Shine Ministries and a charity in the UK called World Shine Foundation, which now has plans to start in the United States as well. We want to support people who are in pain, to prepare for the healing of the nations. We want people to shine for Christ wherever they are in order to bring healing and community transformation.

We started by sharing our vision with people. A man who heard us talk gave fourteen thousand dollars. It was enough to start everything that we wanted to do. We bought land in Rwentobo—in western Uganda, just twelve miles from the Rwandan border—and set up a nursery school, World Shine Foundation School, which could support one hundred children. We put an advertisement out for orphans and needy children, not really thinking we would be oversubscribed. Almost five hundred turned up for registration. We had to find ways of making a selection, all the time cutting the numbers back. It broke our hearts. We finally selected 126 children under nine years old who were in desperate need.

The children were taught in an old building, and the next year we added another class. Then another, and another. We now have almost five hundred pupils, ranging from two- to twelve-year-olds. We have almost two hundred orphans, some of whom have lost parents to HIV/AIDS, others to malaria or other sicknesses, and others to domestic violence. The community where the school is located is predominantly Islamic, and polygamy has a hold on people. Sadly the community oppresses women, and we find that a female child is heavily disadvantaged. And yet God smiles on what we do. We have over seventy Muslim students who are happy to join us as we study in a Christian setting, using Christian materials.

We feed our students physically as well as spiritually. We offer two meals a day, which makes a significant difference in an area where malnutrition is so prevalent. Our twelve teachers also undertake outreach work with the children, finding out where they live and trying to improve conditions for them.

We work with families to help them break free from extreme poverty. We have a *send a goat* project, where supporters can pay for a goat to be given to a family in need. These little animals provide milk, kids, and much-needed meat. We are planning a *send a chicken* program as well, and no matter what you may have heard about these programs, I can assure you that when they are run as ours is—with actual goats being given to actual families—the impact of these simple projects is incredible.

We also encourage people to sponsor our students. At the moment a little fewer than half our students are sponsored, at a cost of fifteen dollars a month. That amount provides scholastic materials, two meals each day, and a uniform. Part of it goes to what we pay the teachers (who get paid eighty-five dollars a month), and our aim is to grow to provide accommodation for those children who come from violent homes, or total orphans and other children at risk. Last year one parent killed his wife in front of his child—a student of ours. We would like to build an orphanage where they could stay in the same place they learn, and where we would know that the mattress and blankets that we have given are being used by the children themselves, not by a parent who should know better.

Every child writes to his or her sponsor every term. And we encourage the sponsors to write back, to send gifts and the like at Christmas and the child's birthday. Sponsors receive term reports, and we encourage them to come and visit the children, to see them at school and even in their homes.

We also support widows in Rukungiri, Connie's hometown. We work with women who have lost their husbands to HIV/AIDS and support them and their children, giving them goats and money for agriculture. We support other widows in eastern Uganda with goats and money to set up home businesses. They form small groups that meet during the week to decide what economic microenterprise project they want to start and then deliver. Some choose to invest in livestock; others make other plans. But the end result is always the same: Lives are changed, and eventually communities are transformed. We also have a radio program in my hometown of Kabale that is used for advocacy for women and children in communities where many people cannot read and have no access to television.

Uganda really is a remarkable country. Our past is scarred in pain and our present riddled by corruption, but we have so many wonderful Christians at work among us. The country holds a magnetic appeal for Christians from the West, so much so that at times the flights into Entebbe Airport feel like airborne Bible study groups. But this great work exists only because there is a great need. And if World Shine Ministries was not active in Rwentobo, the village would be sinking deeper and deeper into poverty, ignorance, and disease.

I believe that Christians in the West have a big contribution to make in the development of Africa. Many people say the scale of the problem is too great, but I believe if you educate a child, you have educated a nation. Bit by bit, this transformation can take place, and within fifty years we could transform the entire continent.

You can see the potential in the area around our school. With more sponsors we could build an orphanage to protect the vulnerable children. With extra funding we could set up a clinic to help the community solve its health problems: malaria, dysentery, diarrhea, and all sorts of other preventable diseases that claim the lives of so many women and children. A clinic would allow us to go out to the villages to educate about health, hygiene, water, sanitation, and the importance of immunizing the children. We believe in community transformation because we see it in action.

There are forty thousand orphans in this region who have lost both parents. I believe that in the next ten years this project will help more than ten thousand children, expanding the capacity for primary students and beginning to offer a secondary-school education to those who wish to continue. During the summer months we plan to offer a vocational school so that children who do not do well academically can learn trades such as carpentry, bricklaying, computing, and sewing. With these skills behind them, as well as the knowledge of how to practice good hygiene, all in the context of sound Christian values, how could the future not look radically different?

And if we can help some of the 64 percent of people in the area who are illiterate, if we can teach them to read and write as well as be healthy and self-reliant, what better (and longer) lives they could lead!

I think I have said enough about World Shine Ministries and World Shine Foundation, and I should stop here. Just remember that something special has happened here, that this region so blessed by God with its beauty and its incredible bounty, as well as its history of revival, is not just a place of poverty and desolation. It is a place of life, of great potential, and of profound spiritual wealth.

I have told you about the work of World Shine Ministries because you have already played a part in supporting our work. By buying this book you have helped create much-needed income, and for that I am so very grateful. Thank you. If you have not bought this book, remember this: I was a very good librarian and I know all the tricks people use to get away without paying!

≋

Before we end, permit me to share just a few final thoughts about the type of forgiveness that is at the heart of these pages you hold in your hand. Revolutionary forgiveness changes not only the one who forgives but also the one who is forgiven. And more—the family and surrounding community are affected.

Revolutionary forgiveness brings about a change that affects lifestyle, priorities, and marriages. It goes beneath the surface to alter character, to change your way of life, the people you live with, your community, your thinking, your priorities, your communication. Charisma minus character is very dangerous. Revolutionary forgiveness deals with character.

And we need more of it today. We need it between tribes, between churches, on a personal, village, community, and national level. Even at a racial level we need forgiveness. And we need it between genders.

We need people who will make the choice to forgive wholeheartedly, totally, patiently, indiscriminately, continually, despite pain, without thought for the payback, sacrificially—even though someone does not deserve it.

We need people who are not afraid of the tears, the brokenness, and the chance that they will look like fools. It is painful, and it is continual.

And we need people who crave wisdom. We may end up paying more than others who choose not to forgive, and so we need wisdom. We forgive yesterday, today, until eternity. We shall stop when we die.

≋

If you wish to know the power of revolutionary forgiveness, start by praying this prayer from the bottom of your heart:

Lord Jesus, I thank You for loving me unconditionally.

I thank You for speaking to me in this book about bitterness and forgiveness.

I ask You to forgive me for all my sins and wash me clean with Your blood.

Fill me now with Your Holy Spirit and make me whole.

I forgive all the people who hurt me and wounded my heart—those who crushed my self-esteem.

I forgive them totally and unconditionally in Your name.

I denounce all the bitterness, anger, blaming, and unforgiveness in my life in Your name.

I denounce all demons of hatred, anger, bitterness, blaming, and unforgiveness in Your name.

I denounce all the demons from the water, forests, mountains, deserts, the graves; demons of depression, abandonment, rejection, and vagabondism; and all the principalities and strongholds of bitterness and unforgiveness in Your mighty name.

I receive the blessing of Abraham, Isaac, and Jacob in Your name.

I release myself to the covenant of God, which was sealed by Your blood.

I declare I am delivered from anger, bitterness, and unforgiveness in Your name.

I declare I am a victor, not a victim, a success, not a failure, blessed, not cursed, in Your name.

I cover myself with Your blood and build a wall of fire around myself in Your name.

Blessed Holy Spirit, come into my life, lead me, and make me the person You want me to be.

Thank You, Jesus, for healing and delivering me today.

Thank You, Lord, for saving me and making me whole.

In Your name I pray. Amen!

May God bless you abundantly, exceedingly, and beyond any curse as you work out your response to His mighty call on your life. May you notice the tombstone being rolled away and hear the call of Jesus to leave the grave. May you be inspired to perform the privileged function of Christ's church—helping to roll away the tombstones that trap others so they may walk into the freedom of new life. And as you shed the grave clothes and walk free once more, may you know the life-changing, revolutionary power of forgiveness in your own life today, tomorrow, and forevermore. We know it is "not by might, nor by power, but by my spirit, saith the LORD of hosts" (Zech. 4:6).

Tukutendereza Yesu
Yesu omwana gwendiga
Omusayi gwo gunaziza
Nebaza Omulokozi

Glory, glory to my Savior,
Glory, glory to the Lamb.
Oh! His precious blood has saved me,
Glory, glory to the Lamb.

To God be the glory!
Amen.

Notes

1. Festo Kivengere, *I Love Idi Amin* (Grand Rapids, MI: Fleming H. Revell Company, 1977), 25–26.

2. Ibid., page unknown.

Further Information

You can find out more about us from our website:
www.WorldShineFoundation.org

We can also be contacted at:
World Shine Ministries
PO Box 10262
Kampala, Uganda

Email:
medabirungi@gmail.com
(Yes, the *d* in my first name is left off deliberately.)